The
CHRISTIAN
CHURCH
PLEA

by H. Eugene Johnson

New Life BOOKS

A Division of Standard Publishing
Cincinnati, Ohio
40028

Library of Congress Catalog Card No. 75-12012
ISBN: 0-87239-053-5

CONTENTS

INTRODUCTION

The Christian churches and churches of Christ, as a religious body, began at the final turn of the eighteenth century and opening decade of the nineteenth century. The foundation documents were the *Last Will and Testament of the Springfield Presbytery,* signed in 1804 by Barton W. Stone and five other Presbyterian ministers, and the *Declaration and Address* written by Thomas Campbell in 1809. Campbell proposed "It is the grand design and native tendency of our holy religion, to reconcile and unite man to God, and to each other, in truth and love." The acclaimed "masterpiece" and "fountainhead" of this nineteenth-century reformation is the *Declaration and Address.* Its advocates became the mainstream of the people now identified as the "restoration movement." Upon the "principle of reformation" in this document, Alexander Campbell (son of Thomas) launched the reformers: "on this bottom we put to sea, with scarcely hands enough to man the ship."[1] There were "headwinds and rough seas" for several years as Thomas and Alexander Campbell searched to put these principles into practice. Dozens of valiant men were also in the forefront, marching around the walls of sectarianism with the trumpets of the Lord.

It is startling to discover that the phrase "the plea" does not occur in either the *Last Will and Testament* or the *Declaration and Address.* Yet within a few years this plea became the universal designation for the proclamation of the movement. The thought, however, is present in Thomas Campbell's work. He repeated two phrases: "the reformation for which we *plead"* and "we have *overtured."* An overture is an introductory proposal; a plea is an urgent prayer, appeal, or request. The plea to Thomas Campbell was an urgent appeal to the religious world to restore God's people to "visible scriptural unity."

The groups known as the Christian Connection led by Barton W. Stone, and the Reformers under the leadership of the Campbells and Walter Scott, were united in January 1832. This movement became known properly as the Disciples of Christ and popularly as the "restoration movement" in the middle of the nineteenth century. The advocates of the plea grew in number from 20,000 in 1832, to 1,300,000 members in 1909. Today over 4,000,000 are in groups tracing their heritage to the Campbell-Stone movement. Presently there are three major sections of the movement: The Disciples of Christ who are structured on a local, regional, and national basis; the non-instrumental churches of Christ; and the conservative Christian churches who are sometimes called "Independents."

As we read the literature of the restoration movement, we become aware that expressions of the plea differed from generation to generation and varied among contemporaries dependent upon their theological suppositions. It is proper—perhaps necessary—to ask, "What is the plea for our people today?" In a free association of Christians and churches there can be no authoritative answer. There never was! However, after a century and a half the movement needs to re-examine its practices and proclamations in light of its avowed principles. It is the writer's belief that the principles set forth in the *Declaration and Address* form a valid plea for our day.

The first three chapters—PRINCIPLE, PROCLAMATION, and PRACTICE—are saturated with statements from leaders of the past. This is deliberate. Our people are encouraged to know what has been said about our plea. We have traveled highways and byways for some one hundred and seventy years, and we should know precisely where we have been. Hopefully, after a careful study of the past, we may avoid some of the detours ahead as we seek to discover a better highway to the City of God for twentieth-century travel.

---

[1]*Christian System,* 1836, p. XII.

CHAPTER I

THE PRINCIPLE

EARLY CONCEPTS

Everyone knows that the "brotherhood" is the restoration movement! The subtitle to J. D. Murch's volume *Christians Only* is: "A History of the Restoration Movement." Certainly the plea is restoration of the New Testament church. It may surprise some to know that neither Thomas nor Alexander Campbell nor Barton W. Stone ever published the phrase "the restoration movement." This phrase is a promulgation of the second generation Disciples.

It offended Alexander Campbell to be called a "restorationer."[1] Restoration was only a part of the plea of the founding fathers, and its relationship to the other facets of the governing principle is quite crucial. The word "restoration" appears only twice in the fifty-six page *Declaration and Address.* One occurrence is: "restoration and maintenance of christian unity."[2] Notice that restoration refers to unity here. The

---

[1] Campbell protested in 1826: "Some *religious* editors in Kentucky call those who are desirous of seeing the ancient order of things restored, *"the Restorationers,"* "the campbellites" and the most reproachful epithets are showered upon them because they have some conscientious regard to the Divine Author and the divine authority of the New Testament." *Christian Baptist,* vol. 4 (Nov. 1826), p. 88.

[2] *Declaration and Address* and *The Last Will and Testament of the Springfield Presbytery* (Indianapolis: International Convention of Disciples of Christ, 1949), p. 43.

Campbells identified their movement as the "current reformation" or the "present reformation." This use of the word, "reformation," was not a thoughtless choice, but signified the Campbells' acceptance of the idea of "Christendom." Their efforts were a continuation of the "ecclesiastical pilgrimage" commenced by the sixteenth-century reformers. In August 1809, Thomas Campbell formed the Christian Association of Washington (Penn.) with the "sole purpose of promoting simple evangelical christianity." In the *Declaration and Address* he saw this purpose as being accomplished when the denominations would "restore unity, peace and purity to the whole church of God."[3] To Thomas Campbell the plea was for restoration of the vital life of the primitive church, not structure and doctrine. The key thought was using the Bible alone to produce fellowship, spirituality, and catholicity.

The principle propounded by the Campbells and their associates was bound up in the nature of the church, its mission, and ministry. The church of the nineteenth century in free America could be a harbinger of the millenium. How could it accomplish its God-given mission? The Campbells reasoned:

1. *Evangelism is the main purpose of the church.*
2. *Christian union will cure the denominational divisions hindering evangelism.*
3. *Christian union will be produced by a return to the ancient order, a restoration of the New Testament church.*[4]

S. M. Martin of Seattle endorsed this view in his sermon at the 1909 Centennial Convention at Pittsburgh:

> *The two prominent aims of the current Reformation have been, first, the conversion of sinners, and second, the restoration of the lost unity of the church.*[5]

---

[3] *Ibid.*, p. 3.

[4] Alexander Campbell stated his thesis: "Nothing is essential to the conversion of the world but the union and co-operation of Christians. Nothing is essential to the union of Christians but the Apostles' teaching or testimony." *Christian System,* 1840, p. 107.

[5] *Centennial Convention Report 1909* (Cincinnati: Standard Publishing, n.d.), p. 510.

That last phrase, "the restoration of the lost unity of the church," contains a vital point. The Campbells were not "restorationists" as such, because restoration was a method not a goal. Recall the phrase in the *Declaration and Address:* "restoration and maintenance of Christian unity." Thomas Campbell was not thinking primarily of restoring church polity, gospel ministry, or doctrine. His emphasis was to restore the unity of faith and practice that the world might be saved.

Restoration, then, was not the final objective of the Reformers (the Campbell wing of the movement). The objective was world evangelization, obtainable through a particular plea and a program. The plea was unity; the program was restoration of primitive Christianity.[6] The Reformers and Christians at the opening of the nineteenth century faced a "spirit of dogmatism, ecclesiasticism, and sectarianism." They responded with a "spirit of liberty, equality, and fraternity."[7] Nothing less would prepare Christians for their task which was to evangelize, or convert people to the Christ. This was to be done by the church from the launching platform of its "visible unity" of "faith and practice." But this was not seen as *church* union, or a union of denominations. The phrases customarily used by the Campbells were: "christian unity," "christian union." Alexander did use the phrase "church union" once in the 1835 "Preface" and once in the 1839 "Preface to the Second Edition" of the *Christian System.* Such usage was quite rare, for the Campbells' purpose was to prepare the way for a "permanent scriptural unity amongst christians."[8] Proposition 10 of the *Declaration* stated:

> That division among christians is a horrid evil fraught with many evils. It is antichristian, as it destroys the visible unity of the body of Christ.[9]

---

[6] P. J. Rice described the Disciples' position: "It was, therefore, idealistic, practical and purposeful. It presented a great plea, a fascinating program and a glorious objective." *Ibid.*, p. 412.

[7] *Ibid.*, p. 411.

[8] *Declaration and Address,* p. 19.

[9] *Ibid.*, p. 17.

Thomas Campbell understood the prayer of Jesus in the seventeenth chapter of John as God willing unity. If God wills unity, then our complacent disunity partakes of sin. To the Campbells this was not a plea for recognition of the Spirit residing within a Christian (subjective spirituality), the "guarantee" (arrabon) given to all who accept Christ. Jesus' prayer was for visible unity in faith and order, life and work. Its practicality was to be evident. Thomas Campbell described several types of unity that he was *not* advocating: "ecclesiastical unity," "unity of understanding," "unity of sentiment." Ecclesiastical unity would necessitate church union and hierarchical control—an organizational approach. Unity of understanding and sentiment would involve the opinions and personal inclinations of the people. To be effective, unity must have a discernable nature, founded upon objective criteria. Unity is based on faith in Jesus Christ. All else is non-essential.

There were important connotations in the insistence of the Campbells that they were a reformation. One reforms what is already in existence. Christians were in the denominations. There is theological significance in the slogan "We are christians only, not the only Christians." Again, if one is a reformer, he starts within the group. The movement addressed itself at first to the divided church. This was of great priority, for the nature of the church was that it "is essentially, intentionally and constitutionally one." This meant to Thomas Campbell that the church of Jesus Christ is united by its essential nature, by the will of God, and by the content of the Scriptures. Campbell was impressed by the Constitution of the United States of America, written only two decades prior. The church could appeal to the final authority of the divine Word. This thought influenced Thomas Campbell and undergirded his repeated phrase of the "constitutional unity" of the church.

Restoration, as the sole plea, may imply that something is marred or destroyed and not presently available in its essence. Again the purpose of restoration need not be that of unity, as seen today in the approach of the non-instrumental Churches of Christ. However the spirit of restoration is germain to all true reformation. A reform to be effective goes back to the beginning. The early nineteenth-century Disciples were restoring to unite, to save a lost world. The relationship of unity and restoration is important. W. E. Garrison has a point:

> *It makes a world of difference whether a group of restorationists is looking for grounds on which to* separate *or for grounds on which to* unite. *(emph. supp.)*[10]

The Reformers saw themselves as a continuation of the sixteenth-century reformation within the fold of Protestantism, but having the unique advantage of proclaiming the gospel in free America.

Barton W. Stone also thought in terms of reformation at the beginning of the nineteenth century.[11] However, neither Stone nor Thomas Campbell was successful in reforming from within their own presbytery and synod. Both had naively assumed that all clergymen were as amenable to the will of the Lord as were they. Denominational exclusiveness was the style of that day and found expression through allegiance to the Confession of Faith. The presbytery's argument against Richard McNemar (Stone's associate) centered around the proposition of taking either the Bible or the Confession as the true guide. McNemar was bold enough to say the Bible alone is the guide. He preached that "a poor sinner must believe in Him, and that he was capable to believe from the evidences given in the gospel." Without knowing of McNemar's stand, Thomas Campbell strongly emphasized this point in Proposition 3 of his Christian union overture:

> *Nothing ought to be inculcated upon Christians as articles*

---

[10] W. E. Garrison, *Christian Unity and Disciples of Christ* (St. Louis: The Bethany Press, 1955), p. 84.

[11] In a letter written in 1804 to their congregations, five preachers who signed the *Last Will and Testament* (Dunlany, McNemar, Stone, Thompson and Marshall) declared: "We do not desire, nor do we consider ourselves to be separated from the Presbyterian Church, as christians, whether ministers or people, . . . it is not our design to form a party." Barton W. Stone, *History of the Christian Church in the West* (Lexington: The College of the Bible, 1956), p. 10.

of faith; nor required of them as terms of communion; but what is expressly taught and enjoined upon them, in the word of God.[12]

The unity sought was to be a "scriptural unity." Creeds were unnecessary as they were thought to exceed their "lawful use" and "oppose the unity of the church, by containing sentiments not expressly revealed in the word of God."[13] Thomas' satisfaction as a leader came "in vindicating the claims of the Bible as the only rule of faith and practice."[14] The Campbells continued through the years with a reliance upon the Scriptures.[15]

To Thomas Campbell, Biblical unity that cried for restoration was two-fold: faith and practice. Campbell knew the relationship between belief and character. There could be no Scriptural unity without purity. Conduct was to be restored as well as faith. Therefore, as to the subjects of this united "church upon earth," none were to "be retained in her communion longer than they continue to manifest the reality of their profession by their tempers and conduct."[16] We in the twentieth century have sought to restore the unity of the

---

[12] *Declaration and Address*, p. 16.

[13] *Ibid.,* p. 25.

[14] Richardson, *Memoirs of Alexander Campbell* (Cincinnati: Standard Publishing), vol. I, p. 402.

[15] Robert Richardson, Alexander Campbell's biographer and a professor at Bethany College, published a series of articles in the 1852 *Harbinger* which were printed in separate form in 1853 under the title *The Principles and Objects of the Religious Reformation, Urged by Alexander Campbell and Others.* The work begins: "This religious movement is wholly based upon the two great fundamental principles of Protestantism viz:
1. The Bible is the only Book of God.
2. Private judgment is the right and duty of man."
He continued: "But it is unhappily true that the party dissensions of Protestants have insensibly led them to depart, in practice, from both these cardinal principles." This 1853 document is a theological extension to the *Declaration and Address,* and reflects Alexander Campbell's evaluation of the plea when he was 65 years old.

[16] T. Campbell, *Declaration and Address,* p. 18.

primitive church without due concern for the ingredients of "peace and purity," fellowship and character. Thomas was prophetic in understanding that more than doctrine would divide this people. Restoration of the heart precedes restoration of the head if truth is to prevail. Fellowship can stand great stress and diversity in the bonds of Christ's love manifested. Thomas Campbell's plan called for reformation of life, and each congregation was expected to apply the same strict moral code. He reasoned in behalf of unity, "If one church receiving those, whom another puts away, will not be productive of schism, we must confess, we cannot tell what would."[17] He wanted no "unsanctified professors" in this reformation.

The other facet of unit was faith. In the minds of the early brotherhood leaders this was not to be confused with doctrine. Faith was primarily a personal relationship with Christ.[18] Out of this insight came two slogans of the movement. "In faith unity, in opinion liberty, in all things love." The other: "The Gospel is facts to be believed, commands to be obeyed, promises to be enjoyed." Faith is personal. The "facts" involved are the life and teachings of the Master. Commitment to Christ involves the total person, not just his intellect. In the thinking of Thomas Campbell, allegiance to the will of the Master necessitated obedience to the way of the Master—a unity of faith and practice.

---

[17] *Ibid.,* p. 34.

[18] *The Principles and Objects of the Reformation* (an alternate title to Richardson's work) explained the distinction between faith and doctrine: "It (the reformation) seeks to establish a *unity of faith* instead of that *diversity of opinion* which has distracted religious society; and to restore the gospel and its institutions in all their original simplicity, to the world. In brief, its great purpose is to establish CHRISTIAN UNION *upon the basis of* a SIMPLE EVANGELICAL CHRISTIANITY." (p. 2) Richardson continues: "While they (parties) suppose this Christian faith to be doctrinal, we regard it as *personal.* In other words, they suppose doctrines, or religious tenets, to be the subject-matter of this faith, we, on the contrary, conceive it to terminate on a person—THE LORD JESUS CHRIST HIMSELF." (p. 12)

DEVELOPING VIEWS

Thomas Campbell's first intention was to reform from within the Presbyterian denomination and for others to work within their own parties. The *Declaration and Address* was addressed to "our brethren, of all denominations." In 1809, Thomas Campbell believed that all sects held in common the essential core of faith, and differed only by the separate traditions accumulated through eighteen centuries—"the rubbish of ages." He declared:

> *All the churches of Christ . . . are not only mutually agreed in the great doctrine of faith and holiness; but are also materially agreed, as to the positive ordinances of Gospel institution.* [19]

But Campbell erred twice: the denominations did not consider their traditions as "rubbish"; and there was no agreement as to the essence of the ordinances when traditions were subjected to the positions in the New Testament. The Synod recognized that the principles of the *Declaration and Address* were destructive of its creedal and organizational polity and wisely refused entrance to Thomas Campbell and the congregation.

In 1812 Alexander Campbell took over the leadership of the Reformers from his father. Richardson said Alexander had a "more adventurous spirit" and he "could recognize the truth that peace could be reached only through victory." [20] Richardson adds that Alexander had "less reverence for consecrated errors" than Thomas and for remedy preferred the "knife of the surgeon." [21] Everything was to be cut away from the faith that was not authorized by Christ and His apostles. No tradition could be binding without New Testament sanction. On June 12, 1812, the Campbells were baptized by immersion, accepting it as the only Scriptural baptism. Baptism

---

[19] *Declaration and Address*, p. 10.

[20] Richardson, *Memoirs of Alexander Campbell*, vol. I, p. 401.

[21] *Ibid.*, p. 482.

will be examined later on in this work, but it is important to realize that this step was a turning point in Alexander's comprehension of Christianity. Richardson says "it was a discovery which had the effect of readjusting all their ideas of the Christian institution."[22] Most historians have failed to recognize the scope of this change in Alexander's philosophy. [23]

As the Disciples grew from a few thousand to over 300,000 members by 1860, different views were developing as to the nature of the plea. W. E. Garrison and other historians sensed a "temporary eclipse of the union ideal," wherein the plea emerged with a different emphasis:

> The union ideal was now seen in a different perspective. Its realization was seen as linked with, and conditioned by, the success and growth of "our people."[24]

This zeal for "taking the world by storm" was believed by many to be at odds with the original Campbellian position of reformation.[25] The last half of the nineteenth century showed a definite shift in emphasis among many brethren. Thomas Campbell had seen the quest as one of being united in faith and practice, in love and life. As Alexander Campbell developed an organizational position, the accent centered more and more on "the ancient order of things." He pioneered the "Christian system." In the latter half of the nineteenth cen-

---

[22] *Ibid.*, p. 437.

[23] Alexander described this change years later in the 1848 *Harbinger:* "It was not a simple change of views on baptism, which happens a thousand times without anything more, but a new commencement. I was placed on a new eminence—a new peak of the mountain of God, from which the whole landscape of Christianity presented itself to my mind in a new attitude and position." *Ibid.*, p. 344.

[24] Garrison, *Christian Unity and Disciples of Christ*, p. 94.

[25] A. D. Harmon sounded this note of concern at the 1909 Pittsburgh convention. "If other churches do not join our church *en masse*, then do not count the plea a failure. To raise up a great individual people is not our primary mission. This is mere incidental. To produce union is our work. This necessitates a labor with and among other Christians." *Centennial Convention Report*, p. 449.

tury, many writers were producing tracts and pamphlets about the principles and purposes of the Disciples.

J. H. Garrison wrote such pamphlets as: "Our Movement —Its Origin and Aim," "Disciples of Christ, their Purpose, Principles and Progress." W. T. Moore distributed "Our Strength and Our Weakness"; Isaac Errett wrote "Plan of Salvation," "True Basis of Christian Union," "First Principles" and "Our Position." In this latter work Errett wrote of "this plea for a return to primitive Christianity." "Our Position," published in 1872, declares that the "prominent feature" of the plea when first made "to restore the primitive *catholicity* of the church."[26] This is essentially the same message as restoration of the unity of the church, as the unity was to be found in the church's catholicity. Errett distinguished the Disciples' approach from that of the "Broad-church phase" which would develop a "National Church ample enough and liberal enough . . . to meet the wants of all." Also different were "abstract unionists" who regard "*unity* as desirable, but *union* as impracticable . . . a moonshiny sentimentalism of catholicity of *spirit* which they are well assured cannot be realized in *life*"; and the "Organic Union phase" which makes "one big sect out of several smaller ones." All of these approaches "failed to reach the roots of the disease."[27] The Disciples' position, said Errett, was a "doctrine of Christian union" which taught:

1. *Not only the folly, but the* sin of sectarianism.
2. *That unity and union are practicable.*
3. *A return "in letter and in spirit, in principle, in practice" to the original basis of doctrine and of fellowship.*
4. *Where there is no express precept of precedent, the law of love should lead us to that which will promote edification and peace.*

To this Errett concluded: "It cannot be Christian union unless it is union in Christ."[28]

[26] Isaac Errett, *Our Position* (pamphlet) (Louisville: William S. Broadhurst, n.d.), p. 13.

[27] *Ibid.,* p. 15.

[28] *Ibid.,* p. 17.

This linking of Scripture with unity and restoration with unity is important in understanding the plea of the Disciples of the nineteenth century. Brotherhood preachers accepted the Bible as the infallible Word of God, the primitive church as the correct and pure one, and the Church's mission as world evangelization. Two current expressions radically depart from this Campbellian position. The non-instrumental churches of Christ have abandoned the goal of unity, and the Disciples of Christ have abandoned restoration—each because of a different understanding of the purpose and nature of Scripture as to its degree of infallibility and interpretation.[29] To the churches of Christ who accept the New Testament as a detailed blueprint of the church there is only one plea—restoration. To the Disciples of Christ who understand the New Testament as somewhat fragmentary and the primitive church as embryonic, *church* union is the desired end. A spokesman for the structured Disciples of Christ, Ronald E. Osborn, explained that the ecumenical movement cannot

> *accept as sufficient a purely spiritual concept of unity, which rests on individual charity or congregational faithfulness alone and does not deal theologically with the sociological reality of the church as an institution in history.*[30]

A mainstream of thought seemed closer to the developing

---

[29] David Edwin Harrell, a church of Christ scholar, explained the deletion of unity as a goal: "The legalism of nineteenth-century Disciples thought was blunted by a concomitant emphasis on the union of all Christians . . . Disciples did not espouse a detached hope for union; they believed that Christian union was an inevitable consequence of the restoration of the ancient order of things. The two went together . . . Restoration was not an end in itself; it was a means of accomplishing the union of Christians." When the brethren realized the mistake of accenting unity, "The traumatic experience of second-generation Disciples history is the result of the crushing disillusionment that follows the collapse of this dream." David Edwin Harrell, Jr., "Peculiar People." 1966 Reed Lectures. *Disciples and the Church Universal* (Nashville: Disciples of Christ Historical Society, 1967), pp. 38-39.

[30] Ronald E. Osborn, "Witness and Receptivity." 1966 Reed Lectures. *Disciples and the Church Universal* (Nashville: Disciples of Christ Historical Society, 1967), p. 50.

positions of the Campbells: unity and restoration were to remain welded through basic principles of the New Testament church. Robert Richardson closed his work *The Principles and Objects of the Reformation* with this insight:

> That Christian union can be effected by a return to the original principles of the gospel, and in no other way, is, I hope, by this time, sufficiently evident. Simple principles, and not elaborate systems and doubtful opinions, must form the rallying point.[31]

To J. M. Trible the movement was on the march when it flew the flag of faith in Jesus Christ, the flag woven by the apostles. The people were led by the standard that had been carried by the primitive church. There was, however, a difficulty. Trible admitted that there had been "no small disputation among ourselves . . . to find out what is the apostolic teaching, that we may restore it."[32] Perhaps J. W. McGarvey traced the central course of events through several decades when he declared in 1909:

> It was this supreme devotion to the word of God that developed a movement having at first only the union of believers in view, into one having in view the complete restoration of primitive Christianity in its faith, its ordinances and its life, with union as the necessary result.[33]

By the beginning of the twentieth century the plea included a plan of salvation and a special type of church order.

---

[31] Richardson, *The Principles and Objectives of the Religious Reformation* (Bethany, W. Va.: Printed and published by A. Campbell, 1853), p. 45. Herbert L. Willett expressed this idea of "principles" versus that of a "blueprint" restoration thus: "It is not the church life of the primitive years to which the Disciples have sought to point the Christian world, but to the ideals of that church as contained in the teachings of the Master and his Apostles." *Our Plea for Union and the Present Crises* (Chicago: The Christian Century Co., 1901), p. 37.

[32] J. M. Trible, *Trible's Sermons* (St. Louis: Christian Publishing Co., 1892), Reprint, p. 52. Trible further declared, "The principle of the Disciples is the restoration of the primitive and apostolic *faith* to the church, as the only and all-sufficient bond of union." *Ibid.*

[33] *Centennial Convention Report*, p. 381.

It would help to recall the statement of Thomas Campbell as to the purpose of the thirteen propositions in the *Declaration and Address:*

> *To prepare the way for a permanent scriptural unity amongst christians, by calling up to their consideration fundamental truths, directing their attention to first principles, clearing the way before them by removing the stumbling blocks—the rubbish of the ages which has been thrown upon it.* [34]

The movement began for Thomas Campbell in the agony of disfellowship and disunity. For Richard McNemar and Barton W. Stone it was an awareness of the divisiveness of creeds in their erection of "separating walls between Christians." For these and their associates the "standards of faith" that will unite the brethren can only be found in God's divine Word. In a statement much criticized by Alexander Campbell for its assumptions of "restoring the gospel" in 1827, Walter Scott emphasizes the concept of the movement held by its early leaders:

> *At the restoration of the true gospel of Jesus Christ in 1827, nothing except the conversion of the world was more before my mind than the union of Christians. (emph. supp.)* [35]

We can now go back and examine the statement at the beginning of this chapter, that the average member of the movement sees the plea as the *restoration* of the New Testament *church.* This definition is insufficient if it implies that restoration is an end unto itself. It can be misleading if "church" is seen only as structure, organization, or the "ancient order." The statement is erroneous if it carries the idea that everything reported as happening in the primitive church

---

[34] T. Campbell, *Declaration and Address,* p. 19. Seventeen years later this statement appeared in the *Christian Baptist:* "The union of christians it is believed is essential to the glory of God, the happiness of the saints, and the conversion of the world. Jesus Christ is the *foundation* and the *head* of this union, and *faith in him* according to *the scriptural account of his nature and character is the bond of it." Christian Baptist,* vol. 3 (May 1826), p. 193.

[35] *The Evangelist,* reported *The Disciple of Christ, A History,* p. 551.

needs to be reproduced today. Patterns are not identical to principles. If the Campbells talked of a *pattern* in the Scriptures, it was for us to pattern our lives after that of the Master in holiness and purity. Right or wrong, the movement did not begin with a "restoration principle" nor a "blueprint" application, but with a principle of restoring loving fellowship generated by allegiance to the Christ of the New Testament, the source of power for evangelizing the world. I. N. McCash rightly evaluated this principle: "The Restoration movement . . . began in the recognition of and return to the sovereignty of Christ."[36]

---

[36] *Centennial Convention Report*, p. 517.

CHAPTER II

PROCLAMATION

BIBLICAL BASICS

Few mature Christians would decry unity and purity for the church. Restoring the essentials to the body of Christ is a goal few could fault. But how? What procedures should be used in analyzing and interpreting the Scriptures? How is revelation distinguished from relative matters, and through what avenues is it communicated? What import is attached to the traditions of the church through the centuries? To the last question the "founding fathers" answered: return to the Scriptures only, primarily the New Testament. Protestantism had asserted, we too believe in the Bible as our guide, as explained by our creeds. Thomas Campbell viewed the practical situation among the denominations:

> As for the Bible, they are but little beholden to it; they have learned little from it, they know little about it, and therefore depend as little upon it.[1]

The *Last Will and Testament* (1804) suggested a similar ap-

---

[1] Thomas Campbell, *Declaration and Address,* p. 36. For faith, take the Bible alone. Thomas declared: "Is there anything that can be justly deemed necessary for this desired purpose, but to conform to the model, and adopt the practice of the primitive church, expressly exhibited in the New Testament." *Ibid,* p. 10. And, "Nor aught anything be admitted, as of divine obligation, in their church constitution and management, but what is expressly enjoined by the authority of our Lord Jesus Christ and his Apostles upon the New Testament church." *Ibid.,* p. 16.

proach: "We *will,* that the people henceforth take the Bible as the only sure guide to heaven." Thomas' and Alexander Campbell's description of the Bible as "Divine word," "word of God," and "revealed will of God" was neither debated nor denied by their contemporaries. W. E. Garrison believed the context to be

> *Plenary inspiration and biblical infallibility were doctrines having virtually the force of axioms with almost all of them.*[2]

The occasion for the nineteenth-century reformation was corruption of the faith and practice of the church. Negatively attacking corruption will not sustain a reformation, for all lasting movements require a positive base. This base was the New Testament which proclaimed the life and teaching of Christ. To Moses Lard (1818-1880) the "positive element" of the movement was "the determining will of Christ."[3] The will of Christ was personally known by the apostles and prophets; therefore, "the final end to which the reformation should look is a complete return to primitive Christianity in doctrine, in practice, and in spirit."[4] The teachings of Christ and His apostles are correctly known only from the pages of the New Testament. The plea for the all-sufficiency of the Christ of the Scriptures rang out for the dissolution of sectarianism. It established a new direction for Biblical interpretation. Allan B. Philputt declared: "The Bible was a tangled skein until they found the clue. The clue was Christ."[5]

To the early brotherhood leadership, the New Testament was not a book of laws and restrictions primarily, but the revelation of the Son of God. Salvation was not a mechanical process but a personal relationship with the Savior.[6] No one

---

[2] W. E. Garrison, *Christian Unity and Disciples of Christ,* p. 81.

[3] Moses Lard, "The Reformation For Which We are Pleading—What is It?" *Lard's Quarterly,* Sept. 1863, p. 11.

[4] *Ibid.*

[5] *Centennial Convention Report,* p. 388.

[6] A. C. Smither states of Campbell's position: "His claim that the teachings of Jesus as recorded in the Scriptures were alone authoritative was revolutionary in the age in which he lived." *Ibid.,* pp. 385-386.

act or thing was the essence of the relationship with Christ. This was not the opinion of many of the brethren who held that baptism was essential for salvation and therefore for fellowship. In the famous and controversial issues sparked by the "Lunenburg Letter" appearing in the September 1837 *Harbinger,* Campbell replied to the argument that only the immersed are saved:

> *It is the image of Christ the Christian looks for and loves: and this does not consist in being exact in a few items, but in general devotion to the whole truth as far as known.*[7]

therefore

> *There is no occasion, then, for making immersion, on a profession of faith, absolutely essential to a Christian— though it may be greatly essential to his sanctification and comfort.*[8]

The year 1827 was a focal one in proclaiming the plea, for it was the year Walter Scott began his evangelism in the Mahoning Association. He brought to the movement a fresh insight to practical christology. The way to accept Christ was found in Matthew 16:16 and Acts 2:38. The sure and reasonable route was faith, repentance, baptism, forgiveness of sins, and gift of the Holy Spirit. This was Scott's "five finger exercise."[9] At last the Campbells, after 18 years of reformation, had an effective vehicle for their Biblical principles. From this point on, evangelism became a major interest to the Reformers.

---

[7] Alexander Campbell (ed.), *Millennial Harbinger,* 1837, p. 412.

[8] *Ibid.,* p. 414.

[9] After viewing Scott's methods and results, Thomas Campbell wrote: "I perceive that theory and practice in religion . . . are matters of distinct considerations . . . We have long known the former (the theory), and have spoken and published many things *correctly concerning* the ancient gospel, . . . in respect to the *direct exhibition* and *application* of it for that blessed purpose, I am at present for the first time upon the ground where the thing has appeared to be *practically exhibited* to the proper purpose." W. E. Garrison and A. T. DeGroot, *The Disciples of Christ, A History* (St. Louis: Christian Board of Publication, 1948), p. 189.

The reformation needed to clear away the faulty construction of the centuries if it was to build upon a solid basis. Creeds and tradition were to be relegated to the status of opinion. Scholastic theology occupied the thinking of the clergy. The Bible was proof-texted and paraphrased to support the creeds. The "level Bible" approach was quite acceptable, and a clergyman was as apt to prove the way of salvation from Joshua as from the Gospel of John. Sermonizing was often a blend of sociology, philosophy and theology. Figurative and allegorical meanings were sought more quickly than literal understanding of the text. To this the *Declaration and Address* declared: "abstract speculation and argumentative theory take no part, either of our profession, or practice."[10]

The influence of the clergy was too great. Before the church could have the Bible, it seemed necessary to Alexander Campbell to free it from the clasp of the clergy. The clergy assumed they had a divine right of interpretation. The "Kingdom of the Clergy" had to be destroyed so that the kingdom of Heaven could have its proper place. Before there could be unity of the church, Campbell reasoned that the nature of the church must be understood. He devoted much of the periodical *Christian Baptist* (1823-1830) to this task. It was not sufficient to denounce the clergy as "hirelings" and "dumb shepherds." The clergy were part of a system that was itself faulty. Campbell often attacked the wickedness of denominations as a violation of the catholicity of the apostolic church. The *Baptist* struck with theological thunder. Lightning flashed, the lines of combat formed, the fight was on. Alexander Campbell was a scholar and a creative genius. Many who followed his path used his form but failed in his content.[11]

---

[10] T. Campbell, *Declaration and Address,* p. 48.

[11] H. L. Willett reflected: "The *Christian Baptist* in its own day, meeting the issues of its generation, was a strong, timely and respect-compelling journal. Its small modern imitators, who have all its spirit of antagonism with none of its breadth of view or loftiness of purpose, are only grotesque." *Our Plea For Union and the Present Crises,* p. 21.

To the Campbells, who were influenced by John Locke's theory of knowledge and who possessed a deep regard for the Scottish school of common sense, each Bible verse had a practical meaning that could be known by the same process that good literature was understood. Alexander had high regard for the "grammatico-historical" method of interpretation of Moses Stuart (1780-1852) of Andover Seminary. Campbell stated in a lengthy article in the *Harbinger:*

> *That the true sense of the words is the true doctrine of the Bible, is daily gaining ground amongst the most learned and skillful interpreters: in one word, that the Bible is not to be interpreted arbitrarily, is the most valuable discovery or concession of this generation.*[12]

Revelation was a question of fact. Therefore, there were "facts to be believed, commands to be obeyed, and promises to be enjoyed."[13] It was not enough that a practice was "in the Book" to require obedience; it must be "expressly revealed and enjoyed in the sacred standard."[14] This was a matter of faith; all else was a matter of "human inference, of private opinion." Here is suggested the two guiding stars for the journey to unity: Scripturalness and catholicity. Both were needed to get a proper "reading" for those navigating these largely uncharted seas. The distinction was made that unity was not uniformity; that liberty and freedom strode side by side with union. Out of this concept came the famous slogan, modified from that of Rubertus Meldenius: "In faith unity, in opinion liberty, in all things love."

Thomas Campbell, B. W. Stone, and Walter Scott were primarily concerned with the life of faith and purity exhibited

---

[12] Campbell (ed.), *Millennial Harbinger,* 1846, pp. 13-24.

[13] C. L. Loos, born in 1823 and younger companion of Alexander Campbell at Bethany College declared of the early leaders: "They were believers in the Bible . . . They had no doubts about any part of that Bible, from Genesis to Revelation . . . it is God's word, and there lay the granitic foundation upon which this mighty cause has built a future which you see today." *Centennial Convention Report,* p. 322.

[14] Campbell, *Declaration and Address,* p. 31.

upon the pages of the New Testament ("Our return to primitive unity and love").[15] Alexander Campbell was more concerned with fact as fact, truth as truth. The proclamation of this emphasis was "the ancient order of things." Eva Jean Wrather, Campbell scholar, defends Alexander's proclamation of the plea:

> He had the courage to face the fact that, if there ever is a united church, then that church will have to be defined, and defined in terms of its faith, its ministry, its sacraments, its order of worship.[16]

Influenced by the "Christian system" expounded by Alexander Campbell, the movement in the later nineteenth century gave pre-eminence to doctrine and worship, to the neglect of fellowship and ethics. Yet an emphasis in the *Declaration and Address* was for a "life of holiness." "Unsanctified professors" would make, at best, a "skin-deep reformation."[17] This accent upon holiness is in accord with the earliest known name for Christians in the New Testament, "followers of the Way."

To C. M. Sharpe, unity in the church would come "through simple faith in Jesus Christ, without the trappings of a burdensome ecclesiasticism, and without the curse of priestly tyranny."[18] J. J. Haley in his volume *Makers and Molders of the Reformation* declared that the proclaiming of "the Bible alone" became an invitation to union on the basis of our interpretations of certain portions of the Bible. The only solution was

> the divinity and personality of Jesus of Nazareth, the object

---

[15] *Ibid.*, p. 54.

[16] Eva Jean Wrather, *Alexander Campbell and His Relevance for Today* (pamphlet) (Nashville: The Disciples of Christ Historical Society, 1953), p. 13.

[17] Campbell, *Declaration and Address*, p. 52. Again Thomas Campbell emphasized: "A manifest attachment to our Lord Jesus Christ in faith, holiness, and charity, was the original criterion of christian character—the distinguishing badge of our holy profession—the foundation and cement of christian unity." *Ibid.*, p. 36.

[18] *Centennial Convention Report*, p. 204.

of faith, the power of salvation, the foundation of the church, the basis of Christian union, the inspiration of the Christian life, the essence of the Christian religion, constitutes the rallying center of all those in every place who call upon His name.[19]

This coincides with the statement of Isaac Errett in his article, "What is Sectarianism," appearing first in Moore's *Christian Quarterly,* that the plea "advocates the union of all believers on these two considerations: faith in Jesus; obedience to Jesus."[20]

RESTORATION REFINEMENTS

As the pioneers of the movement broke new ground in their study of the Bible alone as the book of faith, they commenced on many trails that were not equally edifying. They had no sure compass through the forest of Biblical interpretation. New attitudes were formed and modified. One such expression was the use of debate to promote the plea. It afforded the people an opportunity for fellowship, provided good publicity for the movement, permitted lengthy expressions of the Disciples' position, and afforded a capsule education for budding preachers. Barton W. Stone was more inclined to avoid debate and controversy than was Alexander Campbell. Stone believed debates could solidify positions, thus hindering openness to new ideas. Religion, to Stone, should liberate one not enslave him to a party position. He proclaimed Spirit union as superior to book union, head union, or water union. Peace would come to Zion when Christians restored the fruit of the Spirit of Galatians 5:22, 23. Stone made an analogy between the game of bandy-ball and religious strife. The permanent value of trying to throw the bandy-ball on the ground of the opponent was no more meaningful than tossing the

---

[19] J. J. Haley, *Makers and Molders of the Reformation* (St. Louis: Christian Board of Publication, 1914), reprint library, p. 87.

[20] *Ibid.,* p. 91.

"heresy ball."[21] He preferred to accent faith through love, and let opinion fall where it may.[22]

In the earlier approach, unity would be ushered in by a "restoration of those elements which constitute the unity of the church of the New Testament."[23] This frankly was not too clear a proclamation. What made the early church unified? Thomas Campbell said it was found in "faith and practice." But Campbell's solution required a scholarly dedication to Scripture that many were unwilling to give. For the preacher seeking a practical answer, it could be found in more easily determined and demonstrated circumstance. Many of the second and third generation Disciples sought a restoration of the primitive church in ordinance, organization, and order. By the 1890's and 1900's the accepted designation was "the restoration movement." Though "unity" was alluded to, it was restoration of the primitive church that was emphasized from the pulpits and in the pamphlets. The original thrust of attempting to reform the denominations had given way to a proselyting from the sects and evangelizing of the unsaved. "No book but the Bible" seemed more prominent than "no law but love." The present generation has yet to give adequate expression to the unity of fellowship demonstrated in the New Testament church.

"Unity" and "restoration" are only words, the pieces of slogans, until they are given definition and direction. Unity of whom and for what? Restoration of what? Are these goals or procedures? There was a concensus among preachers and elders in the movement that the New Testament contained all the revelation necessary for anyone to accept Christ and walk in His way, but there was no concensus as to the implications of this belief. That is, what interpretation do we make from the

---

[21] *The Christian Messenger,* ed. by Barton W. Stone and others. 14 vols., 1826-1845. Published irregularly, vol. VII cf. p. 195.

[22] Stone penned: "Let them hold their opinions; but let them hold them as private property. The faith is public property. Opinions are, and always have been, private property." *Ibid.,* vol. IV, p. 163.

[23] *Centennial Convention Report,* p. 202.

silences, the absence of revelation on a subject? Does the New Testament speak authoritatively on all subjects, or only certain subjects? If not all, are some decisions made by Christians guided by the Spirit? Is the New Testament a complete system, planned as a total unit, absolute in every detail, a *blueprint* of the entire church? Or does the New Testament give us principles that are more accurately described as *imprints* of the Spirit? How do we determine what is faith and what is opinion? We all have the same Bible, so why is there disunity and disagreement over its commands, precepts, and instructions?

The Campbells saw the difficulty in the different approaches to Scripture and different theories of usage. They proclaimed certain principles of interpretation that were generally accepted by the Disciples of Christ of the nineteenth century. The basic insights into Biblical study were the following:

1. *Christianity is a distinct institution, complete within itself; its faith and practice revealed within the pages of the New Testament.*
2. *The Bible is to be interpreted as is any good literature, each verse having a primary meaning that is taken in its practical import.*
3. *Scriptures on a subject should be studied together to arrive at the meaning of a passage whose interpretation is difficult in isolation.*
4. *The Bible reveals a "development of the divine character and government" and it is "essential to distinguish" the (a) patriarchal institution (b) Jewish religion and (c) Christian economy.* [24]
5. *The Christian church commenced its formal existence on the day of Pentecost.*
6. *In conversion the Holy Spirit does not operate separate from the Word of God (an attack upon mourners' bench conversions seeking a Holy Spirit sign of acceptance by God).*

---

[24] Richardson, *The Principles and Objects of the Religious Reformation,* p. 28.

7. *"Nothing ought to be inculcated upon Christians as articles of faith, nor required of them as terms of communion, but what is expressly taught and enjoined upon them in the word of God."*[25]
8. The congregation is the definitive group representing the church, and is, in fact, the local expression of the total church.
9. The distinction between personal faith and doctrinal knowledge.
10. The distinction between faith *in the revelation of Scripture and* opinion *expressed in theology.*

These formed the basis, the approach, to achieving unity.[26]

Thomas Campbell's slogan "Where the Scriptures speak, we speak; where the Scriptures are silent, we are silent," has been too often misunderstood.[27] It meant to the Campbells speaking *authoritatively* concerning the worship, discipline, duties, and government of the church where there is an express command in the New Testament. It meant that Campbell had faith in Christians to act democratically in the spirit of Christ on matters where no command was given, yet where a duty was indicated. Observe the statement in the preface of Alexander Campbell's the *Christian System:*

> The principle which was inscribed upon our banners . . . was, "Faith in Jesus as the true Messiah, and obedience to him as our Lawgiver and King, the ONLY TEST of Christian character, and the ONLY BOND of Christian union, com-

---

[25] T. Campbell, *Declaration and Address*, p. 16.

[26] In addition to the above proclamations Thomas Campbell emphasized:
1. If the Lord gives a command without giving a "manner of performance" no human authority can command the "supposed deficiency." *Declaration and Address*, Prop. 5.
2. Where the Lord "has not enjoined" a command, no "human authority" can "impose new commands." *Ibid.*

[27] J. A. Meng, an opponent of the organ in worship, proclaimed: "The organ is *not* commanded, is *not* prescribed, is not lawful, consequently it can't be expedient, and no one has any right to contend for it in the worship who is willing to 'Speak where the Bible speaks, and be silent where the Bible is silent.' " *American Christian Review*, March 19, 1878, p. 89.

munion, and co-operation, irrespective of all creeds, opinions, commandments and traditions of men."[28]

This accent on faith and truth being related to the person Jesus Christ kept the Campbells from developing a theology of biblicism and verbalism. The Bible was the *Word* of God, but the *Word* of God was personified in Jesus Christ. In this regard the Bible does not take on the significance of an architectural blueprint, committed to unvariable positions not subject to amplification.

DIVERGENCE

Preachers such as Jacob Creath, Jr. (1799-1884), Moses Lard (1818-1880), Tolbert Fanning (1810-1874), Benjamin Franklin (1812-1878), and David Lipscomb (1831-1917) did not accept the distinctions that the Campbells, Walter Scott, Barton W. Stone, D. S. Burnet, and others made between the revelation of Jesus Christ and the revelation of the Bible. These elders were imbued with the fire of the *Christian Baptist;* they were not as sympathetic to the more positive positions advocated in the *Millennial Harbinger.* Jacob Creath believed that Robert Richardson, W. K. Pendleton, and others adversely affected Alexander Campbell after 1849, inasmuch as writings after this date in the *Harbinger* had a more ecumenical outlook. It was largely these differing concepts of Biblical interpretation that began crystalizing the disciples of Christ versus the churches of Christ in the last quarter of the nineteenth century, culminating in the formal separation recognized by the United States Bureau of the Census in 1906.

The leadership of the non-instrumental churches of Christ depreciated the Campbellian proposition that world evangelism can only be effected through Christian union. This segment of the movement became wedded to the sole principle of restoration of a divine blueprint system for the church. Today we see the logical result of this system of verbal inspi-

---

[28] A. Campbell, *Christian System* (1840), p. xii.

ration in the score or so divisions among the churches of
Christ. The statement of L. S. Brigance in the *Gospel Advocate* in 1941 spotlights this strain of pattern philosophy:

> *God gave the world a perfect system of religion at the be-
> ginning of the Christian age, and it cannot be improved. It is
> fixed and permanent. It is inflexible. It is perfectly adapted
> to the needs of humanity in every age. To modify it is to
> impeach the wisdom of God and to usurp his authority. It is
> the sin of presumption.*[29]

There may well be a sin of presumption, but this presumption
is that faith in Jesus Christ is a fixed system of doctrine.

Another segment of thought developed in the 1880's-
1890's, wherein the proclamation no longer included the
necessity of congregationalism or verbal inspiration. W. B.
Blakemore described this development as including "a growing recognition that it is impossible for the church to exist, or
for the gospel to be preached, without any mixture of
philosophy, the tradition of men, or the rudiments of the
world."[30] This element saw the congregational theory as inadequate, but being further solidified by the introduction
about 1910 of the term "local autonomy." W. E. Garrison, says
Blakemore, in the early part of his illustrious teaching career
at the University of Chicago, taught that the definition of the
church as a "voluntary association of believers" was a political doctrine derived largely from John Locke. Garrison believed that it was error for the Campbells to postulate that
union could be achieved through "a definite program of ordinances, worship, and government for the church, all infallibly
derived from the infallible Scriptures and completely uncon-
taminated by 'human opinions.' "[31]

Alexander Campbell in the *Christian Baptist* and early *Millennial Harbinger* years was dedicated to setting up the king-

[29] *Gospel Advocate,* (Dec. 4, 1941) quoted in A. T. De Groot's *The Restoration Principle* (St. Louis: The Bethany Press, 1960), p. 157.

[30] Wm. Barnett Blakemore, *The Discovery of the Church* (Nashville: Disciples of Christ Historical Society, 1966), p. 60.

[31] Garrison, *The Disciples of Christ, A History,* pp. 149-150.

dom in delineating "the ancient order of things." Garrison's criticism of Campbell's "definite program" points up the Campbellian high concept of Scripture as "revelation of faith and duty," as God's "constitution" for the church, and as the "only authentic source of all religious information."[32] Yet Garrison fails to acknowledge the critical approach used by the Campbells, wherein the New Testament read with respect to "proper contextual connection" [33] displayed levels of authority ranging from the life and teaching of Jesus to apostolic "approved precedent." In fact many occurrences in the Scriptures gave rise to opinion and speculation but were not binding upon the Christian. For example, catholicity was in the *practice* of the ordinances of baptism and the Lord's Supper, not their *interpretation.* Isaac Errett, following the thesis of Thomas Campbell, stated that in realizing the ideal church we must guard "against all attempts to coerce unity, either in regard to inferential truths or matters of expediency."[34] The theory of the New Testament church as being pre-cast and handed down complete as a "pattern" is contrary to the Campbells' philosophy of history. It is in violation of the role assigned to the Holy Spirit in Scripture and contradicts the unfolding historical drama clearly exhibited in the New Testament.

In Chapter II of the *Christian System* Campbell discusses the Bible. He makes two statements that clearly release Scripture from the role of a wooden, non-flexible, doctrinal system. "The Bible is a book of facts, not of opinions, theories, abstract generalities, nor of *verbal definitions*," (emph.

---

[32] A. Campbell, *The Christian Baptist* (1824) vol. II, p. 64.

[33] A. Campbell, *Millennial Harbinger* (1839), p. 28.

[34] Haley, *Makers and Molders of the Reformation,* p. 94. J. B. Briney further quotes Errett on this matter: "We will yield to the prejudices and preferences of any and all, and sacrifice all cherished habits, tastes, and expediences. But in regard to the faith and practice revealed in the New Testament, we must be sternly uncompromising." *Centennial Convention Report,* p. 398.

supp.).[35] Again Campbell gives as "Rule 1" in understanding Scripture, *"consider first the historical circumstances of the book. These are the order, the title, the author, the date, the place, and the occasion of it."*[36]

When arguing against mystical Spirit-action upon Christians, Alexander did stress the verbal, the factual, and the logical concepts. Robert O. Fife, professor at Milligan College, has captured the Campbells' best meaning of restoration of the "ancient order of things," as encompassing things both ordered and free. Thus understood, restoration "is the discernment and *reception* of those redemptive and edifying relationships of the *Koinonia* of Christ, offered through the Gospel and portrayed in the order of the early Church."[37] Love and camaraderie are the bonds holding faith and opinion, order and freedom, and discipline and diversity in a workable relationship. The nineteenth century "current Reformation," says Harold W. Ford of Cincinnati Bible Seminary,

> *eschewed personal experience as authority, as well as Roman ecclesiasticism as authority by asserting the absolute and final authority of Jesus Christ, unqualified and undelegated, as contained in Holy Scripture.*[38]

Campbell, Richardson, Pendleton, Errett, and others of their lineage made a distinction between basic Christianity and mature Christianity in proclaiming duty. This is recognition that some things are of the *esse* of the Church, and some the *bene-esse;* that is, some of the *being* and others of the *well-being* of the Church. This position was not accepted by such leaders as Fanning, Creath, Lard, Franklin, and Lipscomb. The distinction related to baptism, as to whether immersion was essential to the *being* of a Christian or to his *well-being.* In the 1837 *Harbinger,* Alexander Campbell de-

---

[35] A. Campbell, *The Christian System,* p. 6.

[36] *Ibid.,* p. 3.

[37] *Disciples and the Church Universal. Reed Lectures for 1966,* p. 19.

[38] *Christian Standard,* founded 1866 by Isaac Errett, Cincinnati: Standard Publishing, (Nov. 26,1972), p. 18.

fined a Christian:

> But who is a Christian? I answer, every one that believes in his heart that Jesus of Nazareth is the Messiah, the Son of God; repents of his sins, and obeys him in all things according to his measure of knowledge of his will. [39]

What then of catholicity and unity? Campbell explains:

> for the sake of union among Christians, it may be easily shown to be the duty of all believers to be immersed, if for no other reason than that of honoring the divine institution and opening a way for the union and co-operation of all Christians. Besides immersion gives a constitutional right of citizenship in the universal Kingdom of Jesus. [40]

The plea, in its virgin power, had been for the denominational world to accept Jesus Christ of the New Testament as the object of our faith, rather than to impose any set of doctrines. It intended to establish clearly the new kingdom and set the boundaries of essentials of faith. It left all other matters to opinion, growth, and development. The proclamation that fundamental faith is personal commitment to Christ and not synonymous with the organizational life of the primitive Church escaped the thinking of many advocates of the plea. The distinction was not maintained as these leaders did not adequately distinguish between restoring the *essential unity* in the New Testament church and restoring the New Testament church per se. The *Declaration and Address* pleaded for the former without insistence upon the latter. Alexander Campbell, by stressing the "ancient order of things," implied that the restoration of the primitive church was the logical and necessary consequence of seeking the unity of the church. Current leadership has not faced this issue adequately.

The Disciples following Campbell's leadership and the Christians following Stone "united" in Lexington, Kentucky, on New Year's Day, 1832. "Raccoon" John Smith, preacher of

---

[39] A. Campbell, *Millennial Harbinger*, (Sept. 1837), p. 411.

[40] *Ibid.*

the Disciples, spoke:

> There are certain abstruse and speculative matters–such as
> the mode of divine existence, and the nature of the
> atonement–that have, for centuries, been themes of discus-
> sion among Christians . . . By a needless and intemperate
> discussion of them much feeling has been provoked, and
> divisions have been produced . . . No heaven is promised
> to those who hold them, and no hell is threatened against
> those who deny them.[41]

Those present understood the warning and prediction: if the
movement could not distinguish between revelation and interpretation, could not live comfortably in the large room of
opinion, then schism would result. When Isaac Errett assumed national prominence as editor of the *Christian Standard* (beginning 1866), he tried to soften the thrust of the
legalists and the developers of detailed plans and procedures
being promulgated as God's infallible plan. Where Alexander
Campbell had accented revelation as factual and rational, Errett emphasized the truth in its relation to human need.[42]

Errett delivered the Missouri Christian Lectures for 1883,
wherein he distinguished between *inspiration* and *infallibility.*
How we know truth, the problem of religious knowledge, was
a concern as it affected the promulgation of the plea.

> Admitting the fact of inspiration, have we in the inspired
> Scriptures an infallible guide? Are they absolutely free from
> error? That all truth is infallible needs no proof. But, is the
> communication of truth, in the inspired Scriptures, abso-
> lutely free from error? I do not see how we can answer this
> question affirmatively unless we can prove that human lan-

---

[41] M. M. Davis, *The Restoration Movement of the Nineteenth Century* (Cincinnati: Standard Publishing, 1913), reprint library, p. 154.

[42] Jessie Brown Pounds gives this appreciation of the application Errett
gave to the Plea: "He contributed also a *spirit of moderation.* He came unto
prominence at a time when extremists and radicals were claiming right of
way. More than any other man, he helped to hold the Disciples true to that
reasonable spirit which had characterized their leaders in the beginning."
Centennial Convention Report, p. 400.

guage furnishes an absolutely certain method of communication between mind and mind.[43]

J. W. McGarvey took the opposite view, that to deny the "infallibility of the Scriptures" is the "essence of rationalism and it is a long stride in the direction of infidelity."[44] In 1893 McGarvey began his column on "Biblical Criticism" in the *Christian Standard.* This "battle over the Book," to use William E. Tucker's phrase, continued for nearly twenty-five years. Higher criticism found advocates in many of the Disciples leaders, as they welcomed this critical approach to the Scriptures. J. H. Garrison, editor of *The Christian Evangelist,* tried to stay neutral, with the eternal result of receiving brick bats from both directions.[45] The issue, "Can we know Absolutes, absolutely?" has remained with the brotherhood to this day. William Robinson, British scholar, and others have sided with Errett, recognizing that to admit man's fallibilities is not to question Divine truth, but to admit the need of reformation in each ongoing generation.

The most prominent exponent of higher criticism was Herbert L. Willett (1864-1944) who received his Ph.D. from the University of Chicago in 1896. He designated the "level Bible" as a "fetish," and verbal inspiration as "impossible." The first observation had already been made by Alexander Campbell; the second was a new thrust. Willett, considered by many of his brethren as a "liberal" tainted from his association with

---

[43] *The Missouri Christian Lectureship,* p. 167. Errett declared: "Any assertion of infallibility as belonging to the inspired Scriptures, must be subject to the limitations growing out of the imperfections of human language, and the uncertainties and perils ever attendant upon materials placed in human custody, and subject, more or less, to the control of ignorance, credulity, prejudice, or superstition. *Centennial Convention Report,* 1909, quoted by Frederick A. Henry, p. 405.

[44] *The Christian,* (June 16, 1881), p. 1.

[45] He wrote in 1899 concerning the position of *The Christian-Evangelist:* "It has, indeed, championed the right of Christian scholars to discover every fact, historical, chronological, or literary, that throws any light upon any book of the Bible and report the same . . . We have never, however, accepted, much less championed many of the *conclusions* of the higher critics."

the University of Chicago, analyzed the New Testament records in a hermeneutical style that he believed to be spiritual progeny of the Campbells. Willett viewed the apostolic church from four perspectives: source, doctrine, ordinances, and spirit. The sources were the Gospels, Acts, Pauline epistles, and Hebrews. The Gospels gave a "spiritual conception" of Christianity; Acts presented it as "organization"; Paul developed it "doctrinally"; and Hebrews examined the church from the stance of a "larger Judaism."[46] Each view had its validity in its "careful adjustment" to the others.

Today, it is a fair comment that the majority of the leadership of the restructured Disciples of Christ accent neither the original plea nor its proclamation when describing the merits of their church. Conceiving the plea to be restoration and its proclamation that of biblicism, the Disciples of Christ view both as an anachronism. *Church* union has replaced Christian unity; dialogue has supplanted proclamation. Denominationalism is no longer a sin, but represents branches upon the tree of the historic church. Critical studies, accenting the sociological growth of the embryonic primitive fellowship, have occupied the thinking of those in the academic chairs.

Ralph G. Wilburn, writing a "Critique of the Restoration Principle," for *The Reformation of Tradition,* sees restoration theology as error. He declares "the historical Jesus now a problem" because the New Testament is only the "church's belief" about Jesus, and "this testimony of faith is not the record to which the actual history would lead."[47] We are left entirely in the dark as to the proof for this bold assertion, that a writing of faith is by definition untrustworthy for history. Wilburn's conclusion is that the "truth of historical relativism," coupled with the unreliability of "missionary books," demolishes any concept of a "simple gospel." There-

---

[46] Willett, *Our Plea for Union and the Present Crises,* pp. 83-90.

[47] Ralph G. Wilburn, "A Critique of the Restoration Principle," *The Restoration of Tradition* (St. Louis: The Bethany Press, 1963), pp. 221-222.

fore, the Bible as "an *authority* has become problematical."[48] These objections are subjective in essence, assuming what the writer would like to prove. They are not convincing when compared with the historical accuracy of the Scriptures.

Of more importance is Ralph Wilburn's examination of Alexander Campbell's concept of the Bible as an "infallible rule," predicated upon the "Lochean epistemology, with its *tabula rasa* idea of the mind."[49] This would be a telling criticism if the essence of the plea were dependent upon "rationalistic biblicism," which declared that for truth "there is no need of interpretation." It has already been shown that the reformation fathers did not follow this line of reasoning into a "blueprint" theory of Scripture, but balanced their epistemology (if faulty) with personal faith in Jesus Christ. Recall that Campbell stated in the preface to the *Christian System* that "The principle" of the Movement was *"Faith in Jesus as the true Messiah . . . the ONLY BOND of Christian union, communion, and cooperation."* The logician in Alexander Campbell influenced his expressions that faith was basically belief in the facts of revelation in the Bible. Here was faith as intellectual, rational assent—a propositional concept. Yet, Campbell surmounted his own logic by expressing faith as ultimate commitment to Jesus Christ.[50]

This concept of revelation as primarily personal, and faith as life commitment to this historic Christ of the Scriptures rises above inadequate philosophy, sociology, or theology of any age. At his best, Alexander Campbell understood the ongoing of the church for each generation. Of "Christ's body, the church," he declared, "Jesus is the head; and the Spirit is the *life* and animating principle of that body."[51]

---

[48] *Ibid.*, p. 222.

[49] *Ibid.*, p. 228.

[50] Garrison explained this factual approach: "The practical application of that intellectualism was to counteract a determined Protestant mysticism." *Alexander Campbell's Theology*, Christian Publishing Co., 1900, p. 226.

[51] A. Campbell, *The Christian System*, p. 11.

The principle of the plea has not remained static; neither has the proclamation. Much has been trial and error as "pioneer souls blazed a path where highways never ran." The boundaries of this small work do not permit a more detailed analysis, decade by decade, of the variations in the proclamation of the plea. Highlights have been touched. The observant reader, through his religious volumes and periodicals, has an adequate expression of the current manifestations of these principles and projections, even though they may not be labeled as such. We know basically where we are. The two great questions are: 1. From where did we come, and 2. Where should we be going? Before we try to answer the second question, let us see what has been the practical application of this plea.

CHAPTER III

PRACTICE

CONGREGATIONAL POLITY AND FELLOWSHIP

A practice that grew in prominence was that of congregational independence. The autonomy of the local congregation has been designated as bedrock for the restoration movement by the Christian Churches and the churches of Christ. Even though the restructured Disciples of Christ have accented regional and national manifestations of the church, they continue to reiterate the powers of the congregation. In 1940, T. K. Smith, a preacher of national reputation, declared that "local autonomy" was the "basic principle of our people."[1] These views have root in the early years of the Reformers.

Thomas Campbell, sensing that the Christian Association was enjoying a feeling of being a "distinct religious body," applied for membership for the Association in the Synod of Pittsburgh in October 1810. He was refused. One of the stated objections was his "countenancing his son to preach the

---

[1] *Christian Standard,* Sept. 7, 1940, p. 894. Writing in the *Standard* for 1969, James D. Murch said of the attainment of unity: "In the *very nature of the polity* of the New Testament church, unity will be achieved in the realm of the Spirit and of freedom of association on the part of individual Christians and *wholly autonomous local congregations." Christian Standard,* Aug. 30, 1969, p. 7.

gospel without any regular authority."[2] Preaching at the semi-annual meeting of the Association the next month (under the announcement of "Alexander Campbell, V.D.S." - Verbi Divini Minister) Campbell responded to the synod's objection that the *Declaration and Address* "tends to establish independent church government" by declaring:

> *Each church had a government within itself, to which it was subject, yet the churches were not so independent of each other but that they stood in a brotherly relation to each other.*

and until the synod proves that the churches of different cities in the Bible

> *managed their affairs by vote, etc. in superior and inferior courts, we consider such conduct as a gross intrusion on the rights of conscience and the liberties of Christians.*[3]

The Washington Association became the Brush Run Church in May 1811, an independent church. Thomas Campbell was appointed elder, Alexander Campbell licensed to preach, and four deacons chosen. On January 1, 1812, Alexander was ordained to the office of ministry. Living in isolation was not the wish of the Campbells, and though Alexander thought that Baptist ministers, as a whole, were "narrow, contracted, illiberal, and uneducated men," he was "better pleased with the Baptist people than any other community."[4] The Brush Run Church joined the Baptist Redstone Association in 1813.

J. J. Haley recalls that there were theological differences between the congregational control exercised by the Disciples' churches and the structure advocated by the Christians following Barton Stone.

> *The Disciples and preachers coming from the Baptist Church were favorable to Congregationalism—even democratic control . . . and this many of the churches practiced at the beginning. Those who came from the Presbyterians and*

---

[2] Robert Richardson, *Memoirs of Alexander Campbell,* vol. I, p. 328.

[3] *Ibid.,* p. 346.

[4] *Ibid.,* p. 440.

this included the Stone party, were in favor of government by an eldership (presbytery) . . . It was found that neither extreme could prevail, and a compromise was made by agreeing to government by an eldership, but the rulings and decisions of the eldership were subject to approval, amendment or rejection by the voice and vote of the people.[5]

However general agreement prevailed on one theme: There was no Scriptural recognition of regional or diocese control. Robert Richardson stated in the *Principles and Objects:* "There is no such thing recognized in Scripture as a bishop over a diocese containing a plurality of churches." A congregation had its own identity and authority.[6] Of similar import is the statement of Moses Lard a century before that "each individual church is in and of itself, and in its own right, independent of all other churches, . . . and that it is responsible alone to Christ."[7] Alexander Campbell's view is more comprehensive than Lard's. The "congregation of God" is

not a community representative of communities, but a community composed of many particular communities each of which is built upon the same foundation, . . . enjoys the same charter, and is under the jurisdiction of no other community of Christians.[8]

[5] *Centennial Convention Report,* pp. 335-336.

[6] A hundred years later Dean E. Walker, president of Milligan College, declared: "When a congregation surrenders any part of its rights or responsibilities, it diminishes the visibility and power of the Church. If such surrendered part be not recovered and restored, the Church cannot propagate itself. It is emasculated." *The Tradition of Christ* (pamphlet), Milligan College Press, n.d., ca. 1963, p. 8. In his pamphlet, *Renewal Through Recovery,* Dean E. Walker explains that "Each local church is a microcosm of the total or macrocosm" (p. 4).

[7] Moses Lard, *Lard's Quarterly,* Oct. 1867, p. 345.

[8] A. Campbell, *Christian System,* reprint, 1836, pp. 55-56. However, these individual congregations are "one kingdom or church of God, and, as such, are under obligation to co-operate with one another in all measures promotive of the great ends of Christ's death and resurrection." *Ibid.,* p. 56. Therefore, "it is indispensable that they have an intimate and approving knowledge of one another, which can only be had and enjoyed in the form of districts." *Ibid.*

Separate congregational "communities" were not to be segregated, were not to live in isolation. Alexander Campbell saw a need of "district" co-operation. Since the apostles "gave no specific directions" for such districts, they "are left to the wisdom and discretion of the whole community, as the peculiar exigencies and mutations of society may require."[9] Campbell adds: "All the *catholic epistles* are unequivocal proof that co-operation is of the very essence of the Christian institutions."[10] Campbell's awareness of the need of cooperation among congregations was not keenly felt by many of his contemporaries. Little evaluation was given to Campbell's statement in 1853:

> As a religious community, we have been in a transition state, and are yet only partially organized . . . We have grown and spread with unprecedented activity, energy and success. But a period has arrived when individual enterprise must yield to public concert and organized effort.[11]

Extra-congregational activities were achieved by the use of conventions, associations, and societies in the nineteenth century. The Reformers' participation in such groups generated opposton from some of the Christian Connection (Stone's fellowship) who looked askance at those endeavors, recalling tendencies of many Baptist associations.[12] Alexander Campbell put his power and prestige behind cooperative meetings and state and national societies. This in itself kept

---

[9] *Ibid.*

[10] *Ibid.,* p. 59.

[11] A. Campbell, *Millennial Harbinger,* 1853, p. 109.

[12] Walter Scott wrote "Brother Stone" in 1827: "It may then be inquired, what propriety is there in your conference or annual meeting? I answer, simply to worship together and strengthen the bonds of union; to receive and obtain information from the different churches, either from their letters or messengers, and attend to their suggestions, . . . attend to ordination, if thought proper, when required by the brethren; to arrange our appointments so as to supply the destitute churches with preaching; and imitate the primitive church by making such requests only as may be proper to set things in order." *Christian Messenger,* Jan. 25, 1827, p. 49.

opposition scattered and disorganized.[13] Campbell argued in a series of articles in the 1831 *Harbinger:* "The only question is, how shall this be done to the best advantage? The New Testament furnishes the principles which call forth our energies, but suggests no plan."[14] Ten years later he said, "I am so deeply penetrated with the necessity of a more intimate organization, union, and cooperation than at present existing among us."[15]

One of Campbell's better statements on the relationships between independent congregations came as a result of thirteen congregations meeting in Wellsburg, Virginia, on April 12, 1834. A discussion arose as to whether such meetings "might endanger not only the independence of the particular congregations, but the very principle of reformation for which we contend." Campbell responded,

> The kingdom of Jesus Christ consists of numerous communities, separate and distinct from each other, and all these communities owe as much to each other as the individual members of any one of them give to all the individual members of that single community of which they are members.[16]

In the February 1843 issue of the *Harbinger,* Alexander Campbell wrote of a hypothetical situation on an imaginary island, Guernsey, where seven congregations, ineffective individually, pooled their resources to form the church of Guernsey. This evoked responses from those believing any organization beyond the local assembly to be unscriptural.

---

[13] This sample of Campbell's criticism of the legalists who opposed all organization indicates why opponents were leery of him during his prime: "I have found a large class of men, professors, too, who will sit for a year rather than rise up crooked: They are conscientious men; but they do nothing right lest they should do something wrong." *Millennial Harbinger,* June, 1838, p. 269.

[14] *Ibid.,* Oct. 1831, p. 438.

[15] *Ibid.,* Nov. 1841, p. 533.

[16] *Report of the Proceedings of a General Meeting of Messengers,* private printing 1834, reproduced in *Millennial Harbinger,* April, 1835, p. 7.

Between 1840 and 1849 some Campbellian preachers began to recognize the need for organizational competence, resulting in the foundation of the American Christian Missionary Society. Preachers, as Tolbert Fanning, Jacob Creath, Jr., and T. M. Henley, were in opposition because the New Testament, being a perfect blueprint for the church, allowed no provision for such an enterprise. Among those in favor of organizations in general, and the missionary society in particular, were Alexander Campbell, Walter Scott, James Challen, D. S. Burnet, Isaac Errett, L. L. Pinkerton, and John T. Johnson. After the War Between the States, David Lipscomb carried on the "battle of the blueprint" in his *Gospel Advocate.* He argued that all supra-congregational ventures were wrong, perhaps sinful. A devout man of singular mind, Lipscomb was unable at times to distinguish between the Word of God and his interpretation thereof. He exhibits a representative stance in his reply to J. W. Higbee who favored liberty's role of opinion:

> *Accept God, Brother Higbee, as the only legislator in the church of God, and discussion and division will cease. Till then God demands the battle shall go on . . .*[17]

A more liberal, expansive view of the church developed between the 1880's and early 1900's led by J. H. Garrison, H. L. Willett, W. T. Moore, L. L. Pinkerton, E. S. Ames, C. C. Morrison, Peter Ainslee, and others. W. B. Blakemore described the scene: "What was becoming clear early in this century was that an exclusive biblical support could no longer be claimed by a strictly congregationed polity."[18]

Blakemore says the last scholarly effort to plead the "1832 concept of the church" within the ecumenical movement was *How To Promote Christian Union,* by F. D. Kershner in 1916. By the early 1930's there was a recognizable division between the conservative disciples and those more progressive as to Biblical authority, the nature of revelation, and the format of

---

[17] *Gospel Advocate,* May 4, 1887, p. 279.

[18] W. B. Blakemore, *The Discovery of the Church,* p. 27.

the church and its ministry. Blakemore's statement in 1966 seems representative of the structured Disciples of Christ, that they have "come to recognize that the church in its essence cannot be understood apart from the concept of development."[19]

The congregational independency of the nineteenth-century Disciples has been communicated in the twentieth century by the phrase "local autonomy," which means strictly, self-government. Such an interpretation has been exercised by congregations of liberal and conservative views. The Disciples of Christ pamphlet *What Brotherhood Cooperation Means* (1963) used this approach to sanction the adoption of open membership. No one has a right to interfere with the decision of the local board as to the requirements of membership. Numerous congregations of the Christian churches and churches of Christ have relied upon this position to bolster their isolation. Neither concept gives adequate expression to Biblical congregationalism.

In one hundred and sixty years the movement has journeyed from Alexander Campbell's view of the kingdom—church with its revealed congregational order to the divine blueprint position of the churches of Christ and to the local—regional—national manifestations of church as expressed by the Disciples of Christ. Both these interpretations seem to arise from the same principles and plea. Obviously this plea is subject to re-examination and re-evaluation. It is of note that the Disciples of Christ who have been vocal in "discovering" that the Campbell-Stone movement was influenced by the political philosophy of John Locke, have naively predicated their restructured denomination after the *pattern* of American *political* life. Disciples spokesmen seem to have compounded the two errors they find most disturbing in the churches of Christ and the Christian churches.

Ronald Osborn views the Disciples' destiny as involved with ecumenical efforts such as the World Council of Churches

---

[19] *Ibid.*, p. 62.

and Consultation on Church Union (COCU).[20] To Osborn and other advocates, the Disciples of Christ is one of the "separated churches" along with scores of others. Christian union is no longer the goal; rather structured church union among the separate denominational disciplines is sought, each group cherishing its own "gifts of the Spirit." The best response to this interpretation is found with that "liberal" C. C. Morrison, who understood "the denomination as the very nub of the problem of Christian unity."[21] Morrison denounced the denominational system in nine propositions. Included were:

> 5. *It provincializes Protestant mentality by erecting barriers against the free flow of Christian thought.*
> 7. *It denies to the local church the Christian status, the breadth of outlook, the spiritual inspiration, and the richness of fellowship which is its birthright as a part of the ecumenical church.*
> 9. *Glorying in its false freedom, denominationalism denies the freedom that is in Christ.*[22]

To the Disciples of Christ position, Dean E. Walker responds that the catholicity of the church "is destroyed by any attempt to furnish it with an order analogous to that of the civil government."[23] The catholicity of the church is expressed through its congregationalism. As to the relation of agencies and associations to the local congregation, Robert O. Fife observes that the problem is solved

> *not by arbitrarily defining a particular set of institutions as "church" . . . but by viewing agencies in personalistic*

---

[20] Osborn writes: "A new ecclesiastical structure has emerged—the council of churches—to express the continuing envolvement of the separated churches one with another . . . A new concept of church union has also arisen which takes seriously the gifts of the Spirit to all the churches in their history." *Disciples and the Church Universal,* p. 50.

[21] Charles Clayton Morrison, *The Unfinished Reformation* (New York: Harper & Brothers, 1953), p. 26.

[22] *Ibid.,* p. 29.

[23] Walker, *Renewal Through Recovery,* p. 8.

terms. They are related to the Church in those persons who by faith are members of the Body of Christ.[24]

The Christian churches still wait for an acceptable practice of congregational interaction that will satisfy the tenets of local autonomy.

THE ORDINANCES
1. BAPTISM

The ordinances of baptism and the Lord's Supper were woven together from the beginning of the Brush Run Church in 1811, when three members refused to partake of the Supper because they had not been Scripturally baptized. Thomas Campbell immersed them without going into the water himself. James Foster did not think it "congruous" that a pedobaptist should be immersing; however, Campbell was certain that it was "unscriptural" to make the mode of baptism a term of communion.[25] The birth of Alexander's first child in 1812, together with his wife's demand for infant sprinkling, forced the Campbells to re-examine the nature and purpose of baptism. The result was that seven members of the Brush Run Church, including the Campbells, were immersed in Buffalo Creek by Baptist elder Henry Luce, accompanied by seven hours of sermonizing by Thomas and Alexander.

Alexander and the Brush Run Church began a fellowship with the Baptist Redstone Association in 1813. By 1816 many of the Baptist ministers were aware that all was not tranquil. The Reformers immersed but differed on the purpose and meaning of baptism, denying the spirit-conversion experience. The Reformers cared nothing for the Philadelphia Confession of Faith, and denied the Baptist concept of a "level"

---

[24] Robert O. Fife, "Christian Unity as Reception and Attainment." 1966 Reed Lectures. *Disciples and the Church Universal,* (Nashville: Disciples of Christ Historical Society, 1967), p. 21.

[25] Richardson, *Memoirs of Alexander Campbell,* vol. I, cf. pp. 371-373.

Bible. Alexander brought some of these tensions to a head in his famous "Sermon on the Law" in 1816. To avoid the publicity of a showdown with the Redstone ministers and perhaps expulsion, Campbell displayed his sagacity by quietly uniting with the new Wellsburg congregation and affiliating this group with the more liberal Mahoning Association in 1823. To the Reformers baptism provided for remission of sin and brought one into fellowship with Christ's people. The Baptists did not adhere to either one of these positions. In spite of the attacks upon his position, Campbell emphatically denied that he believed in "water salvation" or "baptismal regeneration." Only gradually did the Disciples begin to stress the idea that baptism was the initiation rite into the church, thereby recognizing its social and corporate significance, as well as its capacity for witness.

Recall that Barton Stone accepted unimmersed believers into the Christian Connection without "re-baptism." He followed his heart, not his head, and could not make immersion a test of fellowship. Campbell said it should be required, not on the ground of essential salvation, but on the demand of unity of the church and for Christian maturity. The Stone position was sidetracked but never extinguished. As a young minister, William T. Moore (1832-1926) accepted L. L. Pinkerton's position on open membership and practiced it at the West London Tabernacle in England. But he grew more conservative and by 1908 declared open membership to be untenable and unconstitutional. He wrote in a guest editorial in the *Christian-Evangelist:* "No society of any kind can maintain its organic existence unless it is true to the constitution under which it is organized."

American churches have faced the theory and practice of "open membership" since the turn of this century. This practice sometimes called inclusive membership, is the discarding of believer's immersion as a requirement for admission into the church. Its advocates usually administer only immersion to new converts, but upon transfer of membership accept as adequate any form which the transferee has experienced if he is satisfied with it. There are no advocates of open membership among the churches of Christ or the Christian churches. The Disciples of Christ periodically publish emotional articles in their journals encouraging the practice, such as "I am a Disciple, but . . ." in the July 21, 1974, *The Disciple.* Here the climactic argument is "I could not live with my conscience if I were to say to someone, 'I don't believe in your baptism.' " More mature arguments allege that insistence upon immersion is an ungodly attempt to control God's grace and a denial of the once-for-allness of baptism.

The preceding arguments ignore the theological and philosophical consistency of believer's immersion. Basic errors in the philosophy of open membership include assuming: a magical, ritualistic import to baptism; that any rite called baptism by a denomination carries church approval. The conservative asserts that church approval comes from Biblical adherence, not vice versa. The argument for open membership is erroneous when it equates a denial of one's infant baptism as a denial of one's basic Christianity. Alexander Campbell evaluated this in 1837 in his famous reply to the Lunenburg Letter, recognizing that one can be a babe in Christ as well as mature. As it is possible to live without a hand or eye, it is possible to be an incomplete Christian without Biblical baptism. Campbell insisted we are Christians only, not the only Christians. He could not accept the legal argument that immersion is an absolute pre-requisite to receiving the Spirit. He was of the opinion that some "were too much addicted to denouncing the sects and representing them *en masse* as wholly antichristian and corrupt."[26]

Open membership (as well as other concepts endorsed by the Disciples in encouraging COCU) is based on the "branch" theory of the church, which was emphatically rejected by all the nineteenth-century leaders. The Campbells were committed to one, visible church. The *Declaration and Address* exclaims that "division among Christians is a horrid evil fraught with many evils." It is "anti-Christian," "anti-scriptural" and "anti-natural." Isaac Errett said of the convert

---

[26] Richardson, *Memoirs of Alexander Campbell,* vol. II, p. 435.

in baptism:

> He thus lays hold of the promise of Christ and appropriates it as his own. He does not merit it, nor procure it, nor earn it, in being baptized; but he appropriates what the mercy of God has provided and offered in the gospel.[27]

W. E. Garrison expressed the view of many Disciples when he declared: "The adoption of immersion as an essential item in the proposed platform for union radically changed the program of the movement and its relation to the churches which were to be united."[28] The *Declaration and Address* did assume that all the churches in 1809 had a common core of beliefs, union being hindered only by the accumulation of the ages. A fresh study of Scripture soon convinced the Campbells that this was in error. It is also true that requiring immersion was not contemplated in 1809, but returning to primitive Christianity was. Whatever the cost, the Campbells were committed to "obedience to Him in all things according to the scriptures." H. L. Willett complimented Campbell's stance concerning the ordinances:

> They are means of grace to every life. We cannot discard them, nor change them, nor empty them of their significance without being wiser than our Master and thus failing to catch his spirit, which is the essence of the Christian life.[29]

A. L. Haddon, Principal of the College of the Bible, Dunedin, New Zealand, had a novel interpretation of baptism. He believed that the ecumenical movement was unnecessarily pitting infant baptism against believer's immersion, "because of a false identification of the spiritual experience with the symbolic rites which accompany it."[30] It was the error of substituting the "symbol for sacrament." Since baptism encompassed faith in Christ, "neither infant sprinkling nor believer's im-

---

[27] Isaac Errett, *Our Position*, p. 11.

[28] W. E. Garrison, *The Disciples of Christ, A History*, p. 160.

[29] H. L. Willett, *Our Plea for Union and the Present Crises*, p. 108.

[30] Blakemore, *The Challenge of Christian Unity* (St. Louis: The Bethany Press, 1963), p. 68.

mersion is baptism . . . baptism in its full meaning, does not take place at any one moment of time."[31] Thus, to Haddon, infant sprinkling becomes completed baptism with the youth's public confession. There is no need for "re-baptism," as baptism is seen no longer as "two forms of water-rite which are mutually exclusive." The attractiveness of this position pales somewhat when it fails to satisfy the Biblical aspects of the symbol and the spirituality in their *time* relationship. Baptism is a new birth and initiatory rite into the body of Christ. A birth is not a childhood, nor is an initiatory rite a period of probation.

2. LORD'S SUPPER

At the Reformers' separation from the Baptists in 1830, there was no criticism or chant of heresy concerning the Reformers' observance of the Supper. The Baptists restricted participation to immersed believers only. Alexander Campbell accepted this position in the 1830s, and we do not see a pronounced change until his debate with Rice in 1843, at which point he assumed the stance of "let each man examine himself."[32] There was a gradual change among the leadership on the subject of receiving the elements, such that Isaac Errett could remark in the *Harbinger* in 1862 that over two-thirds of the churches declared they "neither invite nor debar."

In the late 1820's and early 1830's there was a difference between the Reformers and the Christians as to administering the Supper. The Christians, following Stone, insisted that only ordained elders should officiate at the Supper. To the Reformers, "there was no exclusive privileges belonging to *preachers* as it concerned the administration of the ordinances."[33] This difficulty was resolved in favor of the Reformers with few overt conflicts and no lasting dissension.

---

[31] *Ibid.,* p. 74.

[32] Garrison, *Christian Unity and Disciples of Christ,* cf. pp. 207-208.

[33] Richardson, *Memoirs of Alexander Campbell,* vol. 2, p. 384.

Isaac Errett spoke for the majority of the progressive Disciples when he commented in 1872:

> The Lord's Supper, too, holds a different place with us from that which is usually allowed to it. We invest it not with the awfulness of a sacrament, but regard it as a sweet and precious feast of holy memories, designed to quicken our love of Christ and cement the ties of our common brotherhood.[34]

In the above, Errett saw the Supper having both individual and corporate significance. This has not been the consensus in the twentieth century. One theology limits the Memorial to individual communion with Christ. W. R. Walker, one-time president of Standard Publishing, wrote to A. T. De Groot:

> "This do in remembrance of me" makes him so central that we may be more or less oblivious to the presence of other communicants. Jesus asked for personal, not corporate, participation.[35]

P. H. Weshimer in his popular tract *Facts Concerning the New Testament Church* agreed with Walker, declaring that the Supper is "not a communion with one another, but with Christ." William Robinson did not accept this personal view as adequate. Pertinent Scriptures included the concept of a church rite (Acts 2:42; 1 Corinthians 10:16-21; 11:20). Those who include a corporate experience reason that if the Supper is one of private communication with God only, why is every reference to it placed in congregational fellowship? And why the insistence upon a loaf being broken to be assimilated by a body of believers?[36] A stimulating treatment of the Supper is

---

[34] Errett, *Our Position*, p. 9.

[35] A. T. DeGroot, *The Nature of the Church*, private printing, 1961, p. 67.

[36] C. C. Morrison understood the Supper to be an expression of Christian unity. "The inherent meaning of this sacramental action of the eucharist is corporate. It is not an action of the individual as such, but a corporate action of the whole church manifested in the local congregation in which each individual Christian participates." *The Unfinished Reformation*, p. 61.

W. B. Blakemore sees the Supper having union significance if understood as a *memorial*, not a *sacrament*. "What needs to be recovered is not Zwingli's idea of remembrance, but the biblical concept of memorial. Secondly, there must emerge an adequate doctrine of the concept of the 'presence' (of God)." *The Challenge of Christian Unity*, p. 92.

furnished by Harold E. Fey in *The Lord's Supper: Seven Meanings.* This 1948 publication evaluates the ordinance as memorial, thanksgiving, covenant, affirmation, spiritual strength, atonement, and immortality.

The American approach of "neither inviting nor debarring" was rejected by the British churches. The British have consistently practiced "close communion" among immersed believers. In 1956 the British Annual Conference adopted the practice of "guest communion," in which a guest would not be questioned as to his baptismal status. The congregation would assume that the visitor was a member in good standing of another church.[37]

THE PATTERN AND THE SPIRIT

The *Declaration and Address* is not a systematic treatise, and there are elements that appear to travel diverse directions. On one hand Thomas Campbell called for a return to "our Lord Jesus Christ in faith, holiness and charity" as the "foundation and cement of Christian unity."[38] On the other, he talked of "taking up things just as we find them upon the sacred page."[39] There was the goal to "realize and exhibit, all that unity and uniformity, that the primitive church possessed, or that the law of Christ requires."[40] However, he declares in one place, "Who would not willingly conform to the original pattern laid down in the New Testament." And again, "Conform to the model, and adopt the practice of the primitive church, expressly exhibited in the New testament."[41]

It is clear, however, that Thomas Campbell in no wise envisioned the New Testament as an architectural blueprint to be followed in every detail with no added procedures. His

---

[37] *Ibid.*, cf. p. 26.

[38] T. Campbell, *Declaration and Address*, p. 36.

[39] *Ibid.*, p. 37.

[40] *Ibid.*, p. 35.

[41] *Ibid.*, p. 10.

"faith and practice" consists of what is "expressly taught and enjoined in the word of God."[42] Campbell states his purpose: "To prepare the way for a permanent scriptural unity amongst christians, by calling up to their consideration *fundamental truths,* directing their attention to first *principles."*[43] Proposition 13 clearly provides for adoption of procedures for the "observance of divine ordinances," under the "title of human expedients."

Alexander Campbell began in the February 7, 1825, issue of the *Christian Baptist* to develop the "ancient order of things." For many years he accented the organization and content of the kingdom, which was then deemed synonymous with the church. Alexander considered this to be the practical application of the plea of the *Declaration and Address.* To him, his plan, his system, logically followed the theory of restoring the unity of the New Testament church. This approach gathered many followers. J. J. Haley believed this phase was not typical of the maturer Campbell and called it "Campbell, number one."

> *Alexander Campbell, Number One, of the covenant theology, the Lochian philosophy and the third epistle of Peter, who stressed the objective in revelation, the external and hence the institutional in religion, begat a spiritual progeny in his own image and after his own likeness, who ran ahead of their maker in a hard, mechanical and quarrelsome legalism.*[44]

At the 1909 Centennial Convention, Miner Lee Bates spoke upon changes and variations in the movement. In areas experiencing less "educational and industrial progress," he

---

[42] *Ibid.,* pp. 10, 16.

[43] *Ibid.,* p. 19.

[44] *Makers and Molders of the Reformation,* p. 82. Haley also saw another Campbell. "There was a prophetic and providential line of lineal descendants from Alexander Campbell, Number Two, of the Millennial Harbinger, Lunenburg letter, and the presidential chair of the American Christian Missionary Society. Men of the type of Isaac Errett, Robert Richardson . . . broadly intellectual as they were broadly spiritual, were in the true prophetic succession from Thomas Campbell and the matured and fully developed Alexander Campbell." *Ibid.,* p. 84.

found that development had followed literal and legalistic avenues.[45]

Two strains began developing in the 1840's and 1850's: A stripping away of every church practice that did not have behind it direct Biblical authority; and an attempt to restore every aspect of the primitive church as foundation to unity. Moses Lard went beyond the Campbellian thought when he declared:

> *That the individual church in its public worship is to be strictly governed by prescription of Holy Writ, or apostolic precedent and that all acts and things not thus sanctioned are innovations and criminal. (emph. supp.)*[46]

The logical conclusion of this blueprint-pattern interpretation has been a legalism where form has replaced substance, letter substituted for Spirit, "phraseology for fact and symbol for the thing symbolized." The fruit of such legalism "is the assumption of finality and self-infallibility which inheres in all its conclusions."[47] There developed substantial differences in

---

[45] Bates said, "Stress is laid upon loyalty to the Word, but sometimes with almost exclusive application to the name, creed, ordinances and organization of the church . . . Denunciation of those varying from this order is seemingly regarded as the highest and holiest duty of the ministry." *Centennial Convention Report,* 1909, p. 437.

[46] *Lard's Quarterly, (Oct. 1867), p. 345.* The blueprint concept shows in Lard's statement in the same article: "When once a *clean riddance* has been made of everything unsanctioned by the Bible, then it was that our plea for union was urged. (emph. supp.) *Ibid.,* p. 342. W. E. Garrison spoke to this trend toward restoration of the primitive Church: "The proposal that the church should be united by treating as essential now only what had been essential in original Christianity represented a valid and fruitful insight. But there were seeds of trouble in an effort to 'restore the primitive church—its organization, worship, doctrine and ordinances.' " *Christian Unity and Disciples of Christ,* p. 211.

[47] J. J. Haley, *Makers and Molders of the Reformation,* pp. 161, 163. The accuracy of Haley's analysis is confirmed by David Edwin Harrell Jr.'s lecture "Peculiar People" at the 1966 Reed Lectures at Nashville: "Any man who believes that he can find literal truth in the Scriptures must also believe that those who do not find the same truth are wrong. What follows is that such people are sinful. The next logical conclusion is that they will go to hell." *Disciples and the Church Universal,* p. 35.

emphasis and attitude between those who accepted Moses Lard's approach and the original thrust for reconciliation in the *Declaration and Address.* Those who espouse pattern restoration interpret "where the Scriptures are silent, we are silent" as an absolute prohibition, instead of the exercise of discretion. There becomes no end of things excluded, no end to proclaiming those differing as "sinful," no end to assigning others "to hell." Leroy Garrett, professor at Bishop College, views such theology with alarm:

> *Lines are drawn on cups, classes, open membership, colleges, congregational cooperation, orphanages, missionary societies, etc. The phenomenal thing about this is that in all these factions you have those who look upon all the others as "walking disorderly."*[48]

These references to the practice of the brotherhood are sketchy, but point up the trends that have been established in proclaiming the plea. The Christian churches have moved from a position of appeal to Christians in the denominations to unite, to the proclaiming of a system of conversion, organization, and ordinances as the restoration of the primitive church. Today unity and union have no immediacy, except as slogans and historical connectives. The sadness, if not the sinfulness, of the current status of the restoration movement is that the vision to heal the divisions of the church has produced a practice of division. If one dared to count, he could come up with about twenty separate fellowships. This shows little receptivity to Paul's admonition to be "eager to maintain the unity of the Spirit in the bond of peace."

The Campbellian concept of unity insisted upon visible unity of the churches, wherein each member or "gospel minister" would have equal fellowship as he journeyed from congregation to congregation. Proposition 2 in the *Declaration and Address* is addressed to the "distinct societies" of the "Church of Christ upon earth." To these *societies* he declares, "there ought to be no schisms, no uncharitable divi-

---

[48] Leroy Garrett, (ed.), *Restoration Review,* private quarterly publication, Denton, Texas, first quarter, 1963.

sions among them." This concept of Christian union is rarely advocated today by proponents of the plea. The most common expression emphasizes unity of individual Christians who have the Spirit. This is seen in Carl Ketcherside's remark: "The unity of the Spirit is a gift of the Spirit to those who have the fruits of the Spirit."[49] Perhaps Thomas Campbell's stress on visible, practical unity, crossing congregational and denominational lines was erroneous, or perhaps it is impractical for the state of christendom in the last quarter of the twentieth century. But if we still believe in the goal of unity, it deserves prayerful analysis and evaluation.

Pattern restoration is more a slogan than a practice among the Christian churches who use the terminology. There remains, however, in the main stream of this fellowship a stress on *verbal* revelation. This emphasis is continued in the Bible college philosophy. Perhaps typical is Article IV of the constitution of the Cincinnati Bible Seminary, setting qualifications for teachers and trustees:

> *To this end every trustee and teacher must be a member of the church of Christ (undenominational) and MUST BELIEVE WITHOUT RESERVATION in the full and final inspiration of the Bible to the extent that it is to him the infallible Word of God, and, therefore the all-sufficient rule of faith and life. (emph. supp.)*

Thomas Campbell used the adverb "infallibly" three times and the adjective "infallible" once in the *Declaration and Address.* The usage: "infallible directory"; "infallibly produce the desired effect"; "infallibly lead to the desired issue"; and "infallibly lead to the desired unity." The contexts are clear that Campbell was using the idea of *reliable,* rather than the concept of incapable of error. If the current usages of *infallible Word* refer to the person Jesus Christ, it comes close to Campbell's theology. If we today imply that the very words of the Biblical text were selected by the Spirit, it is not Campbellian. Hear Alexander:

---

[49] Stanley Paregien (ed.), *Thoughts on Unity* (St. Louis: Mission Messenger, n.d., ca. 1970), p. 186.

Paul says, "We speak spiritual things in spiritual words," or in words suggested by the Holy Spirit. But a very small portion of both testaments are of this character . . . The sense or sentiment of all the sacred books is of divine authority. The words and phrases were in all instances, except in communications purely supernatural, of the selection of the writer.[50]

The apostles, "gifted with a full and perfect knowledge of the Christian institution," expressed the will of God clearly and accurately. Campbell added from his investigation of Scripture, "We are authorized to think that they were as free in the selection of words and phrases as I am in endeavoring to communicate my views of their inspiration."[51]

As legalism became a substitute for Campbellian intellectualism, so in some quarters piety took the place of the Christian life principle. There are habits and traits that obviously run counter to life lived as a temple of God. But preachers, churches, and institutions often added to these a host of activities neutral in themselves. These became a kind of slogan for life, easily identified and classified, such as card playing and theatre going. The conflict presented is that of the Christian versus the world.[52] Moses E. Lard and Benjamin Franklin felt the church was "scandalized" by members who danced and believed discipline was required, even excommunication. A recent example of this pietistic mixture of Christian character and conformity is observed in the matriculation requirements by Memphis Christian College, in its July-August, 1970 "News." Prohibited were not only "the use of tobacco, drugs and improper language," but also "long hair and beards."

---

[50] *Christian Baptist,* 1828, p. 499.

[51] *Ibid.*

[52] Jacob Creath, Jr. wrote concerning the use of tobacco, a description more of semantics than science: "The injurious effects of tobacco are seen in its causing vomiting, purging, universal trembling, staggering, convulsions, languor, feebleness, relaxation of the muscles, great anxiety of mind and a tendency to faint, and blindness." *A Tract on the Use and Abuse of Tobacco,* 1871, p. 6.

The writer is presently wearing a beard (short, neat) but upon self-examination is unable to detect any more sinful tendencies than is normative. Irregularity in conduct, not sartorial dissimilarity, was the concern of the Campbells.

The movement has often failed to distinguish between restoring the New Testament fellowship, and restoring the New Testament form of government. Some of Alexander Campbell's contemporaries viewed his work in the *Christian Baptist* as developing "a particular ecclesiastical order": independence of congregations, dethronement of clergy, weekly observance of the Supper, elders and deacons as the local order of ministry. If made analogous to Ephesians 4, Campbell accented the "one body" and the "one baptism" more than the "one Spirit" and "one hope." As the second generation preachers and editors accented ordinances, order, and doctrine, unity was pushed in the background, receiving only token service. The goal of union became more of a memorial than an objective. Unity was vocalized from the pulpits, but the troops were cautioned to remain at battle stations. The Disciples grew into a major church body and almost ceased talking of *reformation,* proclaiming themselves a *restoration* movement. Even this "watchword" was circumscribed, and the application became an inward focus, a solidifying of concepts of church organization and procedures. The germ of truth was misplaced as many held tenaciously to the shell. This is reflected in the address of Mrs. Louise Kelly of Kansas, at the Centennial Convention in Pittsburgh, who being moved by the progress of the brotherhood exclaimed:

> The machinery of our movement has become so splendidly equipped it may be said we have reached the very flower of perfection in church organization.[53]

Thomas Campbell's insight as to the value of fellowship in achieving the unity of the primitive church has been greatly neglected. John 17 was on his mind at the writing of the

---

[53] *Centennial Convention Report,* p. 444.

Declaration and Address. In Christ's prayer for unity it is noteworthy that this is the only verse in the New Testament where God is addressed "Holy Father." This theme (hagios-holy) is continued in verses 17 and 19 by John's use of the cognate verb "to sanctify" (hagiazein). Holiness is God's special nature. Sanctification "in the truth," holiness in the truth, is part of our unity as we are separated in a salvation fellowship. Sanctification comes from the holy God. Campbell's prayer for visible unity for the church is taken up in his idea of visible fellowship of all the church's members. First a unity of faith and purity. Unity started with each one's sanctification. Campbell phrased it:

> Here we have proposed but one description of character as eligible, or indeed as at all admissible to the rights and privileges of christianity.[54]

There was no hope for unity without "purging the church of apparently unsanctified characters—even of all that cannot show their faith by their works."[55] This seeming harshness is predicated upon the belief that without a sacrificial love for Christ as Lord and Savior, there is not the semblance of the New Testament church.[56] M. M. Davis summarizes this type of unity:

> One final word of much importance remains to be said concerning this union; viz: love was the leading element in this glorious consummation . . . Pieces of steel thrown together will touch each other, but they will not unite; but melt them, and they become one common whole.[57]

---

[54] T. Campbell, *Declaration and Address,* p. 50.

[55] *Ibid.,* pp. 51-52.

[56] Willett expresses the Spirit in the primitive church: "Life became a consecrated thing; the commonest things were dignified and hallowed; the simplest duties were sacraments. It was this new meaning in life which astonished all observers, and made Christianity unique and impressive." *Our Plea for Union and the Present Crises,* p. 110.

[57] M. M. Davis, *The Restoration Movement of the Nineteenth Century* (Cincinnati: Standard Publishing, 1913), reprint library, p. 158.

An 1826 comment on the attitude expressed in the *Christian Baptist* points up a condition that has remained in segments of the movement to this day. A reader known as "RBS" wrote to Alexander Campbell:

> *I have taken the Christian Baptist now from its beginning,
> . . . although sensible and edited with ability, it has been
> deficient in a very important point,* a New Testament spirit.[58]

Whenever the emphasis has been upon "restoring the ancient order of *things*," a severity and harshness has come into the message. When the accent has been upon "restoring the unity and purity of the primitive church," the concern has centered more upon *people* and fellowship.[59] J. J. Haley, sixty years ago, knew the dangers of enshrining doctrine as the solution to disunity:

> *Have we yet to learn that intellectual misconceptions,
> called erroneous doctrines, weigh as light as feathers in
> comparison with the spirit of pride, arrogance, intolerance,
> self-righteousness, and infallible cock-sureness, generated
> by high churches Phariseeism, wherever you find it?*[60]

Legalism produces pharisaism; love produces humility. Legalism is at home in correctness and duty; love lives in grace and peace of mind. Legalism glories in a personal salvation; love seeks joy through fellowship. Legalism is the father of factionism; love is the bond of unity.

UNITY AND RESTORATION

Restoration has its fulfillment in looking backward and forward in a continuing arc, similar to a surveyor lining up his poles to insure the direction of his course. If we are in line

---

[58] *Christian Baptist*, April, 1826, reprint, pp. 177-178.

[59] Lavern Houtz, President of Southeastern Christian College, captures this contrast: "People should be *loved* and *things* should be used. When things are loved and people are used, the result is immoral." *Thoughts on Unity*, p. 136.

[60] Haley, *Makers and Molders of the Reformation*, p. 161.

with the essential faith of the primitive church, then we are moving forward in the path of unity for our day. Everything in the New Testament was not be restored. Scriptures contained "articles of faith" and "divine obligation," which were identified by those concepts "expressly taught and enjoined . . . in expressed terms, or by approved precedent." All else was nonobligatory, described as "opinion." Isaac Errett declared:

> In all matters where there is no express precept or precedent, the law of love should lead us to that which will promote edification and peace.[61]

The *Declaration and Address* made its appeal first to the competing denominations to unite upon their common core of basic Christianity. The appeal fell upon ears too busy to listen. The realization came to the Campbells within a couple of years that there was no common acceptance of what they discovered to be of "divine obligation." There was a new emphasis when the Reformers mobilized as a separate religious group to proclaim that "constitutional unity, peace and charity so essential to Christianity."[62] A third phase began with Alexander Campbell's desire to restore the "ancient order of things." Restoring the New Testament church in organization, doctrine, and ordinance went considerably beyond Thomas' idea to "restore to the church its primitive unity, purity and prosperity."[63] Alexander, however, viewed his efforts as the reasonable path for developing the principles of his father's document. Alexander's thesis is continued in the thought of P. H. Welshimer:

> (Loyal Disciples) are a thousand times more concerned about restoring the church of the New Testament in the whole earth than they are about Christian unity, for when the church of the New Testament obtains everywhere automatically the desired union will be present.[64]

---

[61] Isaac Errett, *Our Position*, p. 17.

[62] T. Campbell, *Declaration and Address*, p. 29.

[63] *Ibid.*, p. 10.

[64] *Christian Standard,* Nov. 5, 1927, p. 863.

In this practice the original twin concepts are taken in succession: restoration followed by true unity. The procedure is to declare the church restored by congregational structure and a three-fold ministry, and invite the world to unite with this complete New Testament church. This formula is too simple. It overlooks the New Testament revelation as to fellowship, stewardship, benevolence, and the functional unity of the body of Christ. Men who follow the "succession plan" without the depth and spirit of P. H. Welshimer need guidance to understand the nature of the church to be restored. When unenlightened restoration became the watchword, the emphasis as to unity "tended to be narrow and provincial." To H. L. Willett at the beginning of the twentieth century, unity seemed to have "no vital relation to our work."[65] Great care is needed to avoid a restoration avenue that runs only into a limited access highway, whose terminal point we do not know. This philosophy seems to say, "We are restoring the church, regardless of where it takes us. When we finish the journey, we shall call the place 'Unity.' " However, unity is not a name transferable to any site in which we reside. Rather, unity is a visible, practical, reasonable, loving relationship between all men who give allegiance to the Christ of the Scriptures. If our journey (restoration) brings us to a place where this type of relationship is not evident, then we have taken the wrong highway.

Catholicity is an outlook that abode with the Campbells. It tempered inclinations toward exclusivism and provincialism. Without this broader view, many proclaimers tended to be right-headed but wrong-hearted. Perry Gresham says this catholicity is not to be confused with sentimentality:

> *Some right-hearted men have been soft-headed. They have been full of love for everyone but had no sound bases in thought and theory for the reunion of Christendom.*[66]

This inclusive view of the church looked beyond the American

---

[65] Willett, *Our Pleas for Union and the Present Crises*, pp. 133-134.

[66] *Thoughts on Unity*, p. 125.

frontier, beyond nationalities to the world church of Jesus Christ unfettered by time and locale. In his debate with N. L. Rice in 1843, Campbell took the catholic position that "all who sincerely believe in the Messiah and are willing to be governed by his precepts" are eligible for His church. Campbell further asserted that "we do not . . . make conditions of ultimate salvation out of the conditions of church membership." This was the issue in the "Lunenburg Letter." Conversely, though immersion may not guard the gateway to Heaven, it is catholic, and therefore the only proper expression for a unity movment.

Preoccupation with restoration in the middle period of Disciples' history, without due thought to catholicity resulted in being "busy digging ourselves into a fixed denominational trench," in the words of William Robinson. In better moments the brotherhood preserved the catholic as opposed to the protestant position, said Robinson in a 1935 address. The movement

> has been Catholic in its emphasis on the sin of the schism: in its high doctrine of the Church as the Body of Christ, . . . in the position which it has given to the two Sacraments of Baptism and the Supper, . . . in the discipline which it has placed on the dogma of private judgment that it should be submitted to the qualified judgment of the Church of all the ages.[67]

Thomas Campbell pleaded for a unity of the church, "as a great visible, professing body, consisting of many co-ordinate associations."[68] This unity was to be evident in the church's "public profession and practice." To Campbell this was a contrast to "ecclesiastical unity." It also encompasses more than that unity that comes with the indwelling of the Spirit to those committed to Christ. Campbell faced the argument that such would be inadequate, as it would be a surface, "external" unity only. This criticism said that with Campbell's plan each Christian could still "entertain his own sentiments."

---

[67] James Gray (ed.), *Towards Christian Union*, 1960, p. 15.

[68] T. Campbell, *Declaration and Address*, p. 30.

Thomas responded:

> Our reply is, if so, they could hurt no body but himself;
> besides, if persons thus united, professed and practiced all
> the same things, pray, who could tell that they entertained
> different sentiments; or even in justice suppose it, unless
> they gave some evident intimation of it?[69]

To Thomas Campbell unity was to be in practice not theory.
Unity in practice permitted diversity in doctrine. Doctrine here
is understood as theology. Alexander Campbell's attack upon
the clergy was rooted in this emphasis upon faith-practice
versus doctrine-theory. The "kingdom of the clergy" had to
be demolished before the return to primitive Christianity
could be effected. Why? Because the clergy dealt in doctrine,
preached theology and philosophy, and performed sociological sermonizing. Without the barrier of the clergy, the people
could return to the faith-fact of Jesus Christ and witness
through the ordinances of the church with purified lives.

In practical churchmanship many in the Christian churches
have ignored Campbell's caution of accenting theology
rather than faith. This is illustrated in a pronouncement by the
minister of a major congregation:

> The church preaches the plenary verbal inspiration of the
> Bible, the diety of Christ, the blood atonement . . . It be-
> lieves in the pre-millennial return of Christ. A strong stand is
> taken against compromising these fundamentals. (emph.
> supp.)[70]

Most of what is declared as fundamentals in this minister's
position would have been described by Thomas Campbell as
"metaphysical speculations," and the minister's insistence
upon it as "a very great evil." Such substitution of theology
(opinion) for faith is a denial of the movement's greatest con-
tribution to unity—no creed but Christ. Such pronouncement
in the name of faith regardless of intentions is theological
biblicism and doctrinal scholasticism. The Campbells main-

---

[69] *Ibid.*, p. 40.

[70] *Christian Standard*, March 10, 1974, p. 5.

tained that truth ultimately was personal not doctrinal. Alexander Campbell, long before C. H. Dodd, stressed the Biblical distinction between *kerygma* and *didache,* preaching and teaching. An evangelist was to "preach the word"; an elder was to be "apt to teach." The preacher proclaimed salvation facts. Therefore, the Campbells would say it is Biblically impossible to "*preach* the plenary verbal inspiration of the Bible."

The Disciples of Christ emphasized a new approach to unity in the second half of the twentieth century. The issue: How do we witness to this need for unity in our present age? The answer: By seeing the goal as *church union,* not Christian unity; by casting off the shackles of the doctrine of restoration. The very "ecclesiastical union" that Thomas Campbell feared has been brought to fruition by the Disciples of Christ concept of "church." "Church" to the current Disciples of Christ leadership is accomplished by uniting some 3,500 congregations into a national order. This order, no longer congregational in essence, declares inherent power in the *regional* and *national* manifestation of church separate from any authority derived from the congregations. This concept of union by itself is actually provincial, for "church" is not the catholic church of Jesus Christ. A proper inquiry is: What unique faith, what special manifestation of the Spirit comes to regional associations per se? What additional sovereignity of the Lord is achieved, granted, or displayed? The Disciples of Christ have become in their journey a denomination dedicated to denominational union, as best exemplified in the aims of the Consultation of Church Union (COCU). As to inherent authority in regions, national assemblies, and councils, Dean E. Walker declares:

> Under no system of Church polity . . . is the essential structure of the congregation possible of elimination nor of neglect . . . The people of God are His children. They learn to regard Him as father in thecontext of family life. This context is impossible save in a local visible communion of believers whose concern for one another can be exhibited in the

With a common aim, a
actice and spirit of humil-
sm and organization—a
son of Overdale College
nnual Conference of the

and we must regather
owing all the richness
octifying of the plea to
and not satisfying our-
sks of the plea—its
t to do.[3]

tion should pass through
e, consolidative, and re-
demonstrate this. The
eative; Errett, Lipscomb,
century has been a con-
ripe for a reformation, a
we do not assume the
al evaluation of our posi-
on. Without penetrating
of our own image. The
tively easy to tread upon.
ose out of condition, is
and spirit may be just as
ectively, cannot claim the
hat ought the plea to be?
uild?

amount of attention to
is undisputed that the
Baptist, Millennial Har-
e the creative thrust for
ne cannot know the plea
re caution is needed.
rilliant pioneer, he was a
argely circumscribed by

n, p. 16.

context of their intimate ordinary day by day lives.[71]

This chapter has evaluated some basic practices and manifestations of the movement, predicated upon its proclamations. This analysis could be carried further into such areas as
education, missions, colleges, ministry, benevolence, and the
nature of the church. Enough has been examined to show
that brotherhood practices have been diverse, and at times,
contradictory. This is not so much a cause of despair as it is
recognition of the expressions freedom took in dissimilar cultural, economic, and theological climates. J. J. Haley had this
realization:

> So long as we strive to actualize the originals, to realize the
> ideals of the inspired Christianity of the New Testament, we
> safeguard our religion from stagnation, open the road to
> perpetual progress, and thus forestall the necessity of
> further efforts at reformation.[72]

The Campbells began their "current Reformation" by breaking new ground, attempting new practices that more clearly
reflected the divine purposes expressed in the New Testament. But each such pioneering exposes one to situations
that generate feelings of frustration and inadequacy. Because
it is human nature to seek security and rely upon custom,
each generation is tempted to rest upon the pioneering of the
past. This we must not do. Therefore we "examine ourselves"
humbly seeking God's will for us for our day.

---

[71] Walker, *The Tradition of Christ*, p. 8. To this thesis, Dean Walker has
contrasted the "tradition of Christ": "a definite commission He gives to His
people, a tradition which cannot be reformed, changed or substituted without denying His lordship and thwarting His mission." *Ibid.*, p. 7.

[72] Haley, *Centennial Convention Report*, p. 336.

CHAPTER IV

PROJECTIO

are not a sect or a denomination
common organization, a common p
ity, we can be a growing organi
movement. Principal William Robir
stated in his 1935 address at the A
British Churches:

> Our plea is really a workable plea
> around the strength of this faith, a
> which has been gifted us in the fr
> manifest itself in each congregation
> selves merely with the dry h
> shibboleths—as we are so often wor

History illustrates that an organiza
four phases: creative, interpretativ
formative. The Christian churches
Campbells, Stone, and Scott were c
and others interpreted; the twentiet
solidation of positions. The time is
re-evaluation of the original plea.
responsibility of a vigorous and criti
tion, we will soon be a denominat
self-analysis, we become a prisone
quicksand of scholasticism is decep
Vigorous exercise, especially to th
often painful. Stretching our minds
painful, but we, individually and coll
title of "temple of God" without it. W
Upon what foundation should we b

This study has paid an inordinat
Thomas and Alexander Campbell.
*Declaration and Address, Christian
binger,* and their other writings we
the movement for over forty years. C
without knowing the position. H
Though Alexander Campbell was a
child of his culture with his thinking

What should be the state of the church in th
the twentieth century? Where should the Chr
be at this stage of their history? After viewing
sions of the plea, its proclamation and pract
one hundred and seventy years, who would be
enough to claim the solution for this generatic
will be in the *consensus gentium,* the share
serious students of the movement. Nothing w
until the need is felt to ask questions, and the c
depend upon attitudes. Courage is a majc
courage to tell the people that restoration is
Honesty is needed—the integrity to admit our
is necessary—to contritely seek forgiveness fo
tions and pride. Love is essential—for withou
sion of Christ we are nothing.

J. H. Garrison placed the proper emphasi
scribed the "distinctive task" of the brotherh
took the solution of that problem of all the
turies, namely: the harmonization of Christi
Christian union."[1] Eighteen years later Edwin
this challenge:

> If our plea for unity means anything at all, it mea
> are obligated to prove to the Christian world that
> can maintain their essential unity in Christ, and

[1] J. H. Garrison, *Christian Union* (St. Louis: Christian Pub
p. 135.

[3] James Gray (ed.), *Towards Christian Uni*

the theologies and philosophies of his day. This also is true of the other religious pioneers. To honor the memory of the founding fathers is to be as creative for our generation as they were for theirs. Were the Campbells alive today, the writer is confident they would modify several of their positions due to the advances in Biblical studies and the explosions of knowledge we have witnessed. Movement or denomination? The choice is ours.

THE WORD OF GOD AND THE WORD OF GOD

It is a universal trait to react strongly to matters that we believe to be dangerous to our faith. Such was the case when the Disciples began. On a frontier accenting Biblical mysticism and evangelistic emotionalism, the Reformers' reaction was understandable, rely on the verbal truths in the Scriptures. This is rational, reasonable, and responsible. From this assertion, it is only a small step to describe the Bible as inerrant and infallible. To the nineteenth-century Christian who viewed verbal statements as facts and who considered the mind a blank slate (*tabula rasa*) upon which is written our visual experiences, it was natural to designate the Bible as the Word of God. A word is a word. The Bible being God's Book must be God's Word.

Many voices in the theological world today depreciate the historical witness of the New Testament. These voices confidently teach the embyronic nature of the primitive church, drawing a parallel between the primitive and developed church and the egg and the flying bird. Fundamentally the plea depends upon a high concept of Biblical authority, inspiration, revelation, and the normative nature of the primitive church. However, we have overreacted often to the position we term "liberal" and "modern" by enhancing the Bible with attributes of our eternal God and Christ. Our response cannot be made in nineteenth-century words. The educated man of our times is not conditioned by nineteenth-century rationalism. He is aware of the problems of knowledge; he understands communication and its interpretation. He realizes that there is interaction between God's abiding truth and cultural vehicles that carry its message. To distinguish the eternal from the temporal, the concerned Christian asks of each Scriptural passage: "What does it say in its setting? What did it mean for its original hearers? What import does it have for my culture? And how may it best be expressed?" To fail to explain the Scriptures may be as detrimental as "explaining away" the Scriptures.

Serious students of Scripture will search the Scripture and not rely upon theories and systems. We can start with the New Testament usage of the term *logos,* word. Examples: "In the beginning was the Word and the Word was God" (John 1:1), "preach the word" (1 Timothy 4:2), "the word of God abides in you" (1 John 2:14), "to hear the word of God" (Acts 13:44), "the living and abiding word of God" (1 Peter 1:23), "that word is the good news which was preached to you" (1 Peter 1:25). These representative selections demonstrate that the *logos* (word) of God is essentially what God said and did for man—God's revelation. God's primary revelation is Jesus Christ. His words become His works, all being the Word. Second, the preached story of the "good news" is the Word of God. Third, the Word is the written message of the Christ, the Scriptures.

For the movement to accept the responsibility of calling "Biblical things by Biblical names," it must have the courage to speak more definitively of the Word of God. We should distinguish between the living Word, Jesus Christ; the spoken Word of God, the *kerygma;* the written Word of God, the Scriptures. Only with the recognition do we understand the slogans of the movement: truth is personal, not doctrinal; and no creed but the Christ. The 1974 International Congress on World Evangelism was held in Lausanne, Switzerland, being attended by some 4,000 evangelicals from more than one hundred and fifty nations. The Congress published *The Lausanne Covenant,* and the expressions under the heading "The Authority and Power of the Bible" are surprisingly re-

context of their intimate ordinary day by day lives.[71]

This chapter has evaluated some basic practices and manifestations of the movement, predicated upon its proclamations. This analysis could be carried further into such areas as education, missions, colleges, ministry, benevolence, and the nature of the church. Enough has been examined to show that brotherhood practices have been diverse, and at times, contradictory. This is not so much a cause of despair as it is recognition of the expressions freedom took in dissimilar cultural, economic, and theological climates. J. J. Haley had this realization:

> So long as we strive to actualize the originals, to realize the ideals of the inspired Christianity of the New Testament, we safeguard our religion from stagnation, open the road to perpetual progress, and thus forestall the necessity of further efforts at reformation.[72]

The Campbells began their "current Reformation" by breaking new ground, attempting new practices that more clearly reflected the divine purposes expressed in the New Testament. But each such pioneering exposes one to situations that generate feelings of frustration and inadequacy. Because it is human nature to seek security and rely upon custom, each generation is tempted to rest upon the pioneering of the past. This we must not do. Therefore we "examine ourselves" humbly seeking God's will for us for our day.

---

[71] Walker, *The Tradition of Christ,* p. 8. To this thesis, Dean Walker has contrasted the "tradition of Christ": "a definite commission He gives to His people, a tradition which cannot be reformed, changed or substituted without denying His lordship and thwarting His mission." *Ibid.,* p. 7.

[72] Haley, *Centennial Convention Report,* p. 336.

CHAPTER IV

PROJECTION

What should be the state of the church in this last quarter of the twentieth century? Where should the Christian churches be at this stage of their history? After viewing varying expressions of the plea, its proclamation and practice for the past one hundred and seventy years, who would be presumptuous enough to claim the solution for this generation! The answers will be in the *consensus gentium*, the shared ideas of the serious students of the movement. Nothing will be answered until the need is felt to ask questions, and the questions asked depend upon attitudes. Courage is a major ingredient—courage to tell the people that restoration is not complete. Honesty is needed—the integrity to admit our errors. Humility is necessary—to contritely seek forgiveness for our presumptions and pride. Love is essential—for without the compassion of Christ we are nothing.

J. H. Garrison placed the proper emphasis when he described the "distinctive task" of the brotherhood. "It undertook the solution of that problem of all the Christian centuries, namely: the harmonization of Christian liberty and Christian union."[1] Eighteen years later Edwin R. Errett gave this challenge:

> If our plea for unity means anything at all, it means that we
> are obligated to prove to the Christian world that Christians
> can maintain their essential unity in Christ, and be patient

---

[1] J. H. Garrison, *Christian Union* (St. Louis: Christian Publishing Co., 1906), p. 135.

with various differences of opinion as to methods of work-ing.[2]

Union makes us one; liberty makes us free. Restoration insures that the oneness is in the living Word of God, Jesus Christ, as designated in the Scriptures. The writer believes that the unity we seek is broader than methods of evangelism, matters of organization, doctrine, and ceremonies. The plea is larger; the limitations have been within us. "Faith and practice" are still partially unexplored concepts of the New Testament church. Our attitudes and inclinations will determine how we plead today. What follows is not set solutions but suggestions that are believed worthy of examination.

MOVEMENT OR DENOMINATION

Even though noble souls in all three branches of the Campbell-Stone heritage are engaged in dialogue in such endeavors as "Fellowship," it is doubtful that this decade will witness any formal union of these bodies. There does not appear on the horizon of this generation any significant union between the Christian churches and churches of Christ and any denominational party or group. The Christian churches will remain a separated group until the twenty-first century or longer. If we have not succeeded in Christian unity or Christian union, do we fold our tents and steal away? Do we admit that we are another denomination, albeit a Bible-centered one? What concepts permit us to continue using the term "movement"? With one small union and two major schisms with a dozen smaller "separating issues," do we deserve to continue as a separate body?

There is a worthy plea yet unfulfilled, and this idea needs a body structure to actuate it. No apology is needed for our separate existence, provided we are moving forward for Christ and His church. If we have a definite Christian purpose and exhibit an expanding development of this purpose, we

---

[2] *Christian Standard,* vol. 59, 1924, p. 454.

are not a sect or a denomination. With a common aim, a common organization, a common practice and spirit of humility, we can be a growing organism and organization—a movement. Principal William Robinson of Overdale College stated in his 1935 address at the Annual Conference of the British Churches:

> Our plea is really a workable plea and we must regather around the strength of this faith, allowing all the richness which has been gifted us in the fructifying of the plea to manifest itself in each congregation, and not satisfying ourselves merely with the dry husks of the plea—its shibboleths—as we are so often wont to do.[3]

History illustrates that an organization should pass through four phases: creative, interpretative, consolidative, and reformative. The Christian churches demonstrate this. The Campbells, Stone, and Scott were creative; Errett, Lipscomb, and others interpreted; the twentieth century has been a consolidation of positions. The time is ripe for a reformation, a re-evaluation of the original plea. If we do not assume the responsibility of a vigorous and critical evaluation of our position, we will soon be a denomination. Without penetrating self-analysis, we become a prisoner of our own image. The quicksand of scholasticism is deceptively easy to tread upon. Vigorous exercise, especially to those out of condition, is often painful. Stretching our minds and spirit may be just as painful, but we, individually and collectively, cannot claim the title of "temple of God" without it. What ought the plea to be? Upon what foundation should we build?

This study has paid an inordinate amount of attention to Thomas and Alexander Campbell. It is undisputed that the *Declaration and Address, Christian Baptist, Millennial Harbinger,* and their other writings were the creative thrust for the movement for over forty years. One cannot know the plea without knowing the position. Here caution is needed. Though Alexander Campbell was a brilliant pioneer, he was a child of his culture with his thinking largely circumscribed by

---

[3] James Gray (ed.), *Towards Christian Union,* p. 16.

miniscent of the *Declaration and Address.*

> *We affirm the divine inspiration, truthfulness and authority of both Old and New Testament Scriptures in their entirety as the* only *written word of God, without error in all that it affirms, and the only infallible* rule of faith and practice. *(emph. supp.)*

When we acknowledge the nature of Biblical Truth, we can think creatively upon *inspiration* and *revelation.* We need the courage of Isaac Errett, in his 1883 Missouri Lectures, who distinguished between the inspired Scriptures and the infallible Word. Errett honestly faced the problems in epistemology: "The limitations growing out of the imperfections of human language." The Word is God and of God and infallible. The application is by man to man and therefore fallible. No one can accuse Errett of denying the authority or inspiration of Scripture. He believed in the all-sufficiency and alone-sufficiency of the New Testament as the rule of faith and practice. Honesty requires that we admit that we do interpret the infallible Word of God. Our plea is based on the truth as we know it; however, our knowledge can be incomplete. This humility prepares us for new insights and new understandings from the written Word of God. W. B. Taylor spoke wisely two generations ago: "We do not plea for an infallible church nor an infallible book, but an infallible Christ revealing himself in both."[4]

THE MINISTRY

There is a minimum of evaluation of the ministry in the preceding chapters. This is not an indication of its relative value. The writer has evaluated the movement's ministry in detail in another volume. The ministry, as such, was not singled out by Thomas Campbell in proclaiming the plea in the *Declaration and Address,* but it was a major part of Alexander Campbell's "ancient order of things." Having discovered a

---

[4] *Christian Standard,* 1903, vol. 39, p. 1798.

fixed order of ministry in the Pastoral Epistles, Alexander assumed that such was universal throughout the primitive church. This led him to describe an order of deacons in the sixth chapter of Acts, and the great majority of brotherhood spokesmen have continued this interpretation.[5] Careful exegesis does not sustain this interpretation. In all probability, if the seven had a title it was elder (Acts 11:30).

Campbell was correct in determining that the nature and function of the ministry is inherently connected with the nature of the church. This truth has been impressed upon the denominations in the twentieth century. The nature of the ministry has been a visible barrier to church union since the Lund Conference on Faith and Order in 1952. Because the Campbells denounced all clergy, some have assumed that the Reformers did not advocate a ministry. Alexander's rejection of the clergy was as a *separate class from* the people, not as an *ordered authority* of the people. The burden of spiritual leadership in the congregation was carried by a two-fold ministry of elders and deacons. The *kerygma,* the gospel, was preached at large by the third type of minister, the evangelist. Campbell called this three-fold order "the standing and immutable ministry of the Christian community."[6]

The Christian churches display an awkwardness today when they speak of the ordered ministry. The great majority thinks in terms of the preacher, the associate, and the youth director. Is the elder a minister? The deacon? Are they only "lay" officials? Some of the people call the minister "Elder So-and-So," but they do not imply the Campbellian eldership. These people call their ordained minister "Elder" or "preacher" because they do not know what else to call him. They have been taught that these are the only options. In the last few years several writers have been bold enough to expose this problem with varying solutions.

The Disciples of Christ have declared they have a clergy whose ordination is controlled through the regional authority

---

[5] *The Lookout,* July 14, 1974, p. 6.

[6] A. Campbell, *Christian System,* 1839, p. 60.

of the denomination. Whether Scriptural or not, this group has committed itself to a consistent format of ministry. The non-instrumental churches of Christ have remained primarily early-Campbellian in their concept of the eldership who control all matters of church life not just the spiritual. In this system the preacher (who must be designated "evangelist") is the servant of the eldership. H. Leo Boles frankly states: "For a preacher to rebel against the Scriptural eldership of the church is to rebel against God and his order of organization."[7] The Christian churches have the least-defined position on ministry. They must face the issues involved. If the elders and deacons are an order of ministry, there needs to be an evaluation of ordination. If they are only lay officers, elders and deacons may have as their chief function the assisting of public worship. The nineteenth-century eldership was a ministry of Word, sacrament, and pastoral oversight. Today?

The term "pastor," as a ministerial office has support in Ephesians 4:11, as distinct from apostles, prophets, and evangelists. If Ephesians is a circular letter for the province of Asia as many scholars assert, the office of pastor is given greater significance. J. W. McGarvey favored a "preaching elder" (1 Timothy 5:17), who gave his "whole time to the work."[8] It is acknowledged that at the beginning of the second century, each congregation was governed by a bishop, or pastor-elder, acting as the president of the elders. By the middle of the second century the separate ministries of bishop, presbyter, and deacon were established. The modern day "preacher" has assumed this second-century position of bishop, for which he need not apologize. The term, "pastor," seems the best designation for this service.

A re-study of the Pastoral Epistles can give new insights into the office of evangelist. A reasonable position can be maintained that Timothy and Titus held the position of

---

[7] H. Leo Boles, *The Eldership of the Church of Christ,* private printing, n.d., p. 32.

[8] J. W. McGarvey, *A Treatise on the Eldership* (Murfreesboro, Tenn.: Dehoff Publications, 1962), p. 66.

evangelist (2 Timothy 4:5), being an office of area supervision. Alexander Campbell refused to so identify Paul's companions, calling them special "agents." Arguing in a circle, Campbell stated Timothy and Titus could not be evangelists because they had "general superintendence of the affairs of churches."[9] Others in the nineteenth and twentieth centuries declared the New Testament evangelist to be a special office that can have no successor. This also should be re-examined in the light of present Biblical theology. Area evangelists, as circuit preachers, were among the Disciples beginning with Walter Scott for the Mahoning Association. All of the founding fathers agreed that such an evangelist could form and supervise churches until their local ministry of elders and deacons were firmly established. If such an evangelist was of the desire, he could supervise these new churches for years before declaring them self-sufficient. The overseas mission field is another recognized exception to the movement's original position on area authority. Has anyone ever seriously questioned the practice by American missionaries of supervising for years several mission stations in Africa or Asia?

In spite of Campbell's consistent evaluation of the three-fold ministry and his insistence he was only a bishop, much of his energies were spent as an area evangelist. He toured, debated, published, held "protracted meetings," and gave advice and counsel to the brethren. He even journeyed to Nashville to denounce the minister, J. B. Ferguson, for three nights from the pulpit! Where did he find Scripture to support this vast activity? He never attempted to. Yet, the brotherhood benefited greatly from his supervision, especially in the formative years. In each generation strong leaders have exercised supervisory control over multiple congregations, regions, even asserting national influence. Authors and editors have been the most successful in establishing these "bishoprics." Until the movement has a clearer understanding of its doctrine of the ministry, it will be hampered in its comprehension of the primitive church.

---

[9] A. Campbell, *Christian System,* 1839, p. 63.

B. A. Abbott declared at the Centennial Convention of 1909:

The pulpit is the church's messenger to the ages. It is the way she fulfills her prophetic mission. Preaching is the greatest duty, as it is the greatest power exercised by the church of the living God. The demands for more ministers and for a high standard of excellency in the ministry are good omens.[10]

This call for a "high standard of excellency" has been ignored more often than heeded. In the 1930's and 1940's an anti-intellectualism developed in the ministry of the Christian churches with a resulting disdain for theology. This was a reaction to the misuse of higher criticism by "liberal" brethren. In the minds of many there existed a dichotomy between evangelism and intellectualism. Paul, the apostle, is the best argument that such need not be. Our seminaries and Bible colleges must face this problem and disarm it by the quality of instruction offered.

CONGREGATIONAL INDEPENDENCE

The significance of one attribute of the Campbells has been lost upon many in the brotherhood. It was their need to be a part of a segment of the church larger than the congregation. They would not let the Christian Association of Washington or the Brush Run Church remain in isolation. At the same time that Alexander was proclaiming the principle of congregational independence, he was also saying, "I do not want to be alone." Extra-congregational fellowship was deemed necessary by the Campbells. Recall Thomas' Proposition 1, that "the church of Christ upon the earth is essentially, intentionally, and constitutionally one." He talked of the "visible unity of the body of Christ." He worked for visible inter-congregational associations. Alexander put his philosophy of cooperation and fellowship into these trenchant words:

---

[10] *Centennial Convention Report,* p. 452.

> *This plan of making our own nest, and fluttering over our own brood; of building our own tent, and of confining all goodness and grace to our noble selves, is the quintessence of sublimated pharisaism.*
>
> . . . .
>
> *To back ourselves up in the band box of our own little circle; to associate with a few units, tens, hundreds, as the pure church, as the elect, is real Protestant monkery, it is evangelical nunnery.*[11]

Though the idea presently is not approved by many leaders of the Christian churches, Alexander Campbell favored regional congregational endeavors, not just the cooperation of individual Christians. In the *Christian System* he described the universal church as "a great community of communities—not a community representative of communities, but a community composed of many particular communities." He stated the same idea in the *Harbinger* of July 1834: "The Church is not one congregation, or assembly, but the congregation of Christ, composed of all individual *congregations* on earth" (emph. supp.) Because of this understanding of congregational interaction, the brotherhood leaders called a delegate or congregational convention for 1849. One hundred and fifty-six delegates arrived from over one hundred churches. However, individuals came who desired to participate, so the delegate convention became a mass convention.

In 1869 there was another attempt at a congregational-directed national convention called the Louisville Plan. Basically there would be annual district conventions of messengers from churches, then an annual national convention with business transacted by state messengers. The meeting in Indianapolis in 1870 was attended by eight times more non-delegates than delegates. Again the individuals were invited to participate, and again it became a convention of individuals. The Louisville Plan was practically abandoned in 1875 and formally terminated in 1881. The point is that brother-

---

[11] A. Campbell, *Christian Baptist*, May, 1826, pp. 204-205.

hood leaders of the first generation were concerned with expressing the oneness of the church by collective *congregational* action. Here was the idea of oneness from a plurality of congregations.

Many of the leaders in the brotherhood view the church as consisting of separate, autonomous congregations with regional and national endeavors being carried on by individuals. Because of this belief the movement generally has depreciated all organizations for cooperative missionary, benevolent, and educational enterprises. Moving this idea to a logical extreme, as do most of the non-instrumental churches of Christ, one believes he can participate fully in the church by fellowshiping in a local congregation only. Again this view is pushed to the extreme in one's refusal to take part in any Christian service activity directed by more than one congregation.

It is basic exegesis that the singular term "church" is used in the New Testament to include a group of congregations in a given local area (Acts 5:11; 8:1; 1 Corinthians 1:2). This does not bolster the theology of totally autonomous congregations. The implication is that Christians had intimate fellowship and organization crossing the confines of local meeting places. Again in 1 Corinthians 12:28, as well as in Ephesians and Colossians, Paul speaks of the sum total of all believers in Christ as the church. Here is the idea of total church preceding in the mind of God the idea of local congregations. Certainly the local congregation is indispensable for spreading the Gospel and close fellowship. Yet no single congregation can be all of the body of Christ. Permeating the New Testament is the concept of a Christian being part of the body, the new Israel of God. This people of God incidentally meets in local groups for geographical convenience, but "the church of Christ upon earth is essentially, intentionally, and constitutionally one."

To the writer, "congregational independence" is a more accurate expression than "congregational autonomy." The true meaning should be congregational *theonomy*—under the sovereign will of God. The love of God directs us in our local fellowship and guides us to cooperate with Christians and groups of Christians in other locales. The movement has yet to restore the full meaning of the primitive church. We have sufficient scholars who can give us fresh insights into participation in the body of Christ.

THEOLOGY AND INTERPRETATION

Alexander Campbell, the movement's great theologian, declared that he would have nothing to do with "the abstract and metaphysical dogmas" of the theologians. This has been wrongly taken as an attack upon theology per se. Theology is merely a study of God, Christ, and His church. Theology is an ordering of our faith. Paul, the apostle, was insistent upon the concept of growth, and the writer of Hebrews urged that we "leave the elementary doctrines of Christ and go on to maturity" (6:1). Theology should be seen as meat of the faith, as added vitality and vision to our basic beliefs. We place theology in the realm of opinion, as interpretation of God's revelation. Maturity insists upon liberty of expression for opinions. Writing in the *Christian Messenger* of January 1832, Barton W. Stone recalled the historic meeting of the Reformers and Christians at Georgetown on New Year's Day, 1832. "It may be asked, is there no difference of opinion among you? We answer, we do not know, nor are we concerned to know." Isaac Errett, a generation later, is quoted:

> *While insisting on loyalty to Jesus, we must allow every man to be loyal to himself in all things not expressly commanded or taught, and regard this liberty as his right and not as our gift.*[12]

One way to "go on to maturity" is through a representative religious journal. The brotherhood does not have presently a vehicle for expressing current theological insights. A people as expansive as the Christian churches cannot afford to be

---

[12] *Centennial Convention Report,* p. 409.

without a journal of mature thinking on the church, her ministry, and mission. We have several national publications, but their format is not such as to accent advance concepts as did the *Christian Baptist* and the *Millennial Harbinger* for their day. Such a monthly journal, if free to express ideas of depth, can have an impact on a wide spectrum of religious people not just our own. In our better moments we know that unity and restoration are vastly more complicated than baptism by immersion, weekly Communion, and local control of congregations. A responsive journal can enhance our understanding of the plea.

The brotherhood needs to be reminded of the interpretations upon which its leadership has relied in formulating positions, particularly the concept of progressive revelation, termed "dispensational authority." The recognition of the different authority inherent in the patriarchial, Jewish, and Christian dispensations, provides the basis for distinguishing between inspiration and authority. This understanding keeps one from succumbing to the "level Bible" concept. Alexander Campbell declared:

> *All the differences in religious faith, opinion and sentiment, amongst those who acknowledge the Bible, are occasioned by false principles of interpretation, or by a misapplication of the true principles.* [13]

On several occasions Campbell published his "seven rules of interpretation"[14] which he described as of "primary importance." In considering the "historical circumstances," using the "same laws of interpretation" as for good literature, in "ascertaining the point to be illustrated," in interpreting "symbols, types, allegories, and parables," Campbell was breaking ground as a pioneer higher critic. These and other hermeneutical devices are valid today for our people, and they deserve to know them.

Of importance is the modification made to the rule of private interpretation of Scripture. The founding fathers bal-

---

[13] A. Campbell, *Millennial Harbinger,* 1846, p. 13.

[14] *Ibid.,* et. al.

anced their interpretation of Scripture with the consensus of Christian scholarship on the subject. The Campbells were influenced in this *consensus gentium* by the Scottish School of Common Sense taught at Glasgow. Knowing this interpretative approach, one understands Thomas Campbell's non-authoritarian attitude to Christian unity. This is related to another popular expression of the Campbells, *"vox populi, vox dei*—the voice of the people is the voice of God." Because we are interpreting in our time and circumstance, accompanied by subjective, non-theological influences, we need to listen to others. Related to *consensus gentium* is *consensus fidelium,* the consensus of the faith in the fellowship of the church. The book of Hebrews reminds us that "we are surrounded by so great a cloud of witnesses" (Hebrews 12:1).

The Campbellian usage of *consensus gentium* and *consensus fidelium* expressed their confidence in the body of Christ, the church universal. This is true catholicity. Such is a far cry from the Roman Catholic concept of the church (meaning the hierarchy) interpreting the Bible for the communicants. The Campbells put no trust in councils or ecclesiastical rulings. Their concern was for the enlightened mind of the Christian scholar. Here is recognition of the working of the Spirit throughout the generations of the church. The brotherhood has paid too little attention to the *Paraclete* who "will teach you all things and bring to your remembrance all that I have said to you" (John 14:26).

THE ORDINANCES

One would suppose that nothing more could be said about baptism and the Lord's Supper, after one hundred and seventy years of continual writings. Much of what has been printed has been reaction to excesses or omissions concerning the ordinances. Debate, argument, and heated discussions are not the best foundation for reflective analysis. At least we can be reminded of some of the more important aspects of these ordinances. We need to evaluate the nature of our communing during the Supper. The tendency is to say we either commune privately with the Lord or that we share a corporate experience. There appears to be no theological necessity to make this an either-or position. The majority of the interpretations have accented the individual, devotional position. More should be said for the Supper's value for fellowship.

It has been noted that all references to the Lord's Supper in the New Testament are within a corporate situation. That is, the Christians came together to "break bread." The symbolism of breaking a loaf and partaking is not complete in isolation. The body of the loaf is re-united in the body of Christ partaking. Again, the fellowship experienced is not limited to those physically present. The body of Christ is universal and its catholicity extends beyond the limits of any one generation. Alexander Campbell emphasized the corporate nature of Communion in the *Christian System:*

> *Each disciple, in handing the symbols to his fellow disciple, says, in effect, "you, my brother, once an alien, . . . are now brought home to the family of God. You have owned my Lord as your Lord, my people as your people. Under Jesus the Messiah we are one."*

He concludes with "Blest be the tie that binds, Our hearts in Christian love . . ."[15] The suggestion for our people is that the Supper affords us four relationships: individual devotion and dedication, visible fellowship with the congregation, a sense of unity with the Church around the world, and an awareness that we are a part of the ongoing body of Christ of which the "powers of death shall not prevail against it."

It is unfortunate that many of the congregations mar the symbolism of the body by offering to the people pre-cut, commercial, unleavened bread. These groups do not *break* the loaf in the presence of the people. The reasons are practical and sanitary, not theological. It is somewhat strange that a movement that has demanded the symbolism of a burial by

---

[15] A. Campbell, *The Christian System,* 1839, p. 331.

immersion has been so lax as to the symbol of the *one* body broken for us. Perhaps the accent upon the individuality of the rite has encouraged a toleration of the individual pieces of bread.

Baptism is more than a physical immersion. To this all agree, for otherwise it would become an aspect of works, not faith. The movement has properly accented the individual's re-enactment for himself of the "passion play" of Christ as the convert lays claim to forgiveness of sins. Alexander Campbell phrased it, "To the believing penitent it is the *means* of receiving a formal, distinct and specific absolution, or release from guilt."[16] Campbell's use of "formal . . . absolution" is an important distinction from the theory of *actual* absolution. Here he was more Protestant than Roman Catholic. If actual forgiveness occurs at the moment of immersion, this would result in "baptismal regeneration," which all of the founding fathers rejected. But if only formal forgiveness occurs, is baptism restricted to symbolism? Perhaps we have given fuller expression when baptism becomes a *sign* and a *means* of actualizing forgiveness.

Baptism, therefore, is a climactic aspect of faith. Baptism as faith-response states that the initiation is from God, the working of His grace. This helps us understand the Scripture, "And the *Lord added* to their number day by day those who were being saved" (Acts 2:47). The movement has tended to shy away from seeing the rite as a "means of grace," as evidenced in J. W. McGarvey's treatment of this verse in his *New Commentary on Acts of Apostles.* There is benefit in encouraging faith-humility in the convert preparing for baptism, over against the implication that he is completing *his* steps of salvation. We are recipients of grace in a personal, believing context. The outreach begins with God seeking our redemption, but is not completed unless the recipient is an active partner in the process. Even with the convert's participation, God's grace envelopes the entire process from beginning to end. This was the theology of Walter Scott. The movement

---

[16] A. Campbell, *Christian System,* 1839, p. 67.

today customarily recites the "five steps of salvation" in one of two ways: hear, believe, repent, confess, be baptized; or faith, repentance, confession, baptism, gift of the Spirit. To Walter Scott, God's grace was most evident in the last two, for he declared: faith, repentance, baptism, *remission of sins* and *gift of the Holy Spirit.* The active response from the convert prevents God's grace from being magical. Though Christian churches have shied away from identifying the ordinances as sacraments, the *sacramentum* was originally a military oath of allegiance. In this light we pledge our lives to our King and give our oath never to desert His standard.

The Scripture, "And the Lord added to *their number* day by day those who were being saved," contains a second purpose for baptism; that is, baptism is the initiatory rite into the church. Baptism, like Communion, has a private and a corporate significance. Sins are forgiven in order that the Christian can become a part of a witnessing fellowship. The movement has failed to accent this position. The convert comes into local fellowship with the congregation, the body of Christ at large, and the Church Universal of all times. A practical consequence of this view is to discourage private baptisms. Baptism is a church rite, wherein the convert makes his first witness to the faith.

UNITY, RESTORATION, AND LIBERTY

We should remind ourselves that we are not dedicated to restoring the restoration movement. We are dedicated to the Christ of the Scriptures, and full fellowship in and with the members of His body. The New Testament is our rule and guide. Yet the Scriptures contain many historical references rooted in cultural, political, and sociological bases. For the plea, what is normative and not transitory? As a people we are fairly well agreed that first-century glossolalia, foot washing, faith healing, psalm singing, and holy kiss are not "commands to be obeyed," and thus not items of restoration. We are not as certain about the nature of the ministry, the public-role of women, and cooperative missions. At times we have been too logical and rational. We have dismissed foot washing and the holy kiss, but these were symbols of humility and fellowship. We seem to have thrown out the service with the symbolic water. The point is, in seeking the normative and perpetual elements of the church, we have been guilty of reaction as well as action.

To be the "current reformation" for our generation we are challenged to examine our charts, course, and the set of our sails to see if our goal has been maintained. The writer suggests the following for consideration: Against creeds and confessions of faith we reacted with a dogmatic pietism. To counteract the clergy we relied upon the "priesthood of all believers" to the detriment of the New Testament ministry. To the claims of the presbytery and synod we reacted with an exaggerated congregational autonomy. Contesting scholastic theology, we urged doctrine as the true faith. We decried theology as man-made, but our interpretations were considered as revelation. Obviously we accomplished more than overreaction in becoming a great brotherhood. But many of the courses we have undertaken could have been more carefully sailed.

One particular course calls for examination, the blueprint-pattern philosophy of restoration. Patternism as expressed today is contrary to the better thinking of the early fathers of the movement. It fails to comprehend the processes of knowing and learning, and verbalizes revelation and the Word of God. Patternism declares that all of God's New Covenant and all of Christianity is contained in the commands, examples, and practices exhibited in the New Testament. Implicit in the theory is the assumption that the New Testament encloses all of God's revelation as a divine textbook on salvation and the church, and infallibly communicates eternal truth through the words of Scripture. The inevitable result is legalistic hair-splitting and breach of fellowship. "Blueprintism" results in provincializing the grace and love of God. As a principle, "blueprintism" thwarts the ongoing revelatory role of the

Spirit. It is a denial of the historical development of the canon. "Blueprintism" fosters two types of error: First, it makes negative commands out of silences and constructs theologies on what *isn't* there; second, it absolutizes and universalizes what *is* there. The "organ issue" booms out of silence. The role of women in the church and society has been distorted by this obsession for expansion and universalizing.

Many noble spirits bred on pattern philosophy seek ways to join hands in fellowship. Instead of casting off the system as a worn-out garment, the non-instrumental leader, J. D. Thomas, in his book, *We Be Brethren,* has worked out a complex formula of "the interrelationship of generics, specifics and expedients" as a "scientific method" of utilizing the "pattern principle." Tragically brethren are struggling with Ptolemaic theology, trying to make the spiritual universe revolve around a static Bible.

Patternism's road leads to disunity. Founded upon verbalism and the infallibility of human communication, it logically leads to authoritative deductions and inferences in the name of revelation. Thus the very *opinions* that Thomas Campbell sought to separate from the *faith* have become the sparks that set off the conflagrations. F. D. Kershner said: "I have lived long enough to know the fallibility of knowledge and the infallibility of love." W. Carl Ketcherside gives similar counsel, "Not only is *agape* the foundation upon which unity is predicated initially, but it is the healing balm which closes wounds and removes scars when schism comes."[17]

This rigorous approach to "blueprintism" is not to depreciate the importance of the Scriptures or to minimize their central and essential position for this movement. The very love we have for God's written Word compels us to be true to its intended purpose. When we study the Scriptures themselves, we are forced to see their movement and power. Acts of the Apostles (of the Holy Spirit) gives us a view of the multifarious outpourings of the Spirit in guiding the apostles and the primitive church. The "occasional" nature of most of

---

[17] Stanley Paregien (ed.), *Thoughts on Unity,* p. 188.

Paul's writings and the compilation procedures employed by Luke defy the assertion that the New Testament writers were only instruments in a rote procedure from God. To point out the failure of the philosophy of patternism is not to decry all procedures and patterns that are evident in Scripture. Christian worship, fellowship, and service without some pattern or form would be anarchy. There are psychological and logical sequences of events—as faith, repentance, baptism—that enhance religious experience.

If unity is the destination of the plea, we should be able to recognize it when we arrive. However, the "travel brochures" being utilized by many brotherhood leaders do not present the same picture. There are several descriptions concerning unity and union in the Scriptures, and effort should be made to guard against the tendency to slip from one to the other. Current writers often distinguish between union and unity, asserting that union implies organization and fellowship while unity is a personal completeness with Christ. Thomas Campbell used the terms unity and union interchangeably in the *Declaration and Address.* To Campbell, "christian unity" included a free interchange of members between congregations, with equal access to the Lord's Table. This union was a practical, demonstrable expression of fellowship. It did not rely upon ecclesiastical concessions. This is not the same idea of unity that is urged by W. F. Lown, President of Manhattan Christian College.

> The individual Christian is the unit of unity, and unity comes down from above . . . When each Christian seeks total renewal and restoration in Christ there will be restoration of unity within the body.[18]

An answer is needed to the question: What is the nature of the unity we advocate for the movement today?

The topic heading is "Unity, Restoration, and Liberty" because the three represent balance for the brotherhood. As stated previously, the Disciples of Christ and the churches of

---

[18] W. F. Lown, *The Restoration Movement and Its Meaning for Today,* Johnson Bible College, 1970, p. 79.

Christ both have separated restoration from unity, each taking a different pole. Separation of the concepts has not fulfilled the plea. Ross J. Griffeth in a 1948 letter to Harold W. Ford discussed the relationship of these three words: "When the emphasis is given to *restoration,* the tendency is to restrict the area of liberty"; and "when *unity* is viewed as the most significant factor . . . the tendency is to compromise . . . in belief and practice"; and "where *liberty* is the dominant emphasis, chaos usually follows in the area of practical problems."[19]

The twentieth century has proven Griffeth's analysis to be accurate. Unity, restoration, and liberty share together the force of the plea, as do the legs of a three-legged stool. When one is missing, the brotherhood stool topples over. To further the analogy, the seat tying the legs together is love. Thomas Campbell understood this and used recurringly such expressions as "christian unity and love," "restoration and maintenance of christian unity," and "constitution unity, peace, and charity." Campbell quotes both Ephesians 4:2, 3 and John 13:34 in which the principle thought is love. Love gloves restoration's hand; love constrains liberty's reach; and love purifies unity's fellowship. "Make love your aim." We have both duty and delight in proclaiming the plea in its fullness. The rest is left with God.

---

[19] Harold W. Ford, *A History of the Restoration Plea,* (Joplin, Missouri: College Press, 1952), p. 192.

BIBLIOGRAPHY

BOOKS

Ainslie, Peter. *If Not a United Church - What?* New York: Fleming H. Revell Co., 1920.

Blakemore, William Barnett. *The Challenge of Christian Unity.* St. Louis: The Bethany Press, 1963.

_____. *The Discovery of the Church.* Nashville: Disciples of Christ Historical Society, 1966.

Boles, H. Leo. *The Eldership of the Church of Christ.* Published privately, n.d.

Campbell, Alexander. *The Christian System.* Cincinnati: Standard Publishing, 1839; reprint, second edition.

Centennial Convention Report (1909). Cincinnati: Standard Publishing, n.d.

Davis, M. M. *The Restoration Movement of the Nineteenth Century.* Cincinnati: Standard Publishing, 1913, reprint library.

DeGroot, A. T. *The Nature of the Church,* private printing, 1961.

_____. *The Restoration Principle.* St. Louis: The Bethany Press, 1960.

Disciples and the Church Universal. Reed Lectures for 1966. Nashville: The Disciples of Christ Historical Society, 1967.

Fitch, Alger Morton, Jr. *Alexander Campbell.* Austin, Texas: Sweet Publishing Co., 1970.

Ford, Harold W. *A History of the Restoration Plea.* Joplin, Mo.: College Press, 1952.

Garrison, W. E. *Alexander Campbell's Theology.* Christian Publishing Co., 1900.

_____. *Christian Unity and Disciples of Christ.* St. Louis: The Bethany Press, 1955.

Garrison, W. E., and DeGroot, A. T. *The Disciples of Christ, A History.* St. Louis: Christian Board of Publication, 1948.

Garrison, J. H. *Christian Union.* St. Louis: Christian Publishing Co., 1906.

Gray, James (ed.). *Towards Christian Union,* 1960.

Haley, J. J. *Makers and Molders of the Reformation.* St. Louis: Christian Board of Publication, 1914; reprint library.

Lown, W. F. *The Restoration Movement and Its Meaning For Today.* Johnson Bible College, 1970.

Mayer, F. E. *The Religious Bodies of America.* St. Louis: Concordia Publishing House, 1958.

McGarvey, J. W. *A Treatise on the Eldership.* Murfreesboro, Tenn.: Dehoff Publications, 1962.

Morrison, Charles Clayton, *The Unfinished Reformation.* New York: Harper & Brothers, 1953.

Paregien, Stanley (ed.). *Thoughts on Unity.* St. Louis: Mission Messenger, n.d., ca. 1970.

Panel of Scholars. *The Renewal of Church,* Vol. I: "The Reformation of Tradition," (R. E. Osborn, ed.). St. Louis: Bethany Press, 1963.

Richardson, Robert. *Memoirs of Alexander Campbell.* Vol. I and Vol. II, reprint, Cincinnati: Standard Publishing. Original, Philadelphia: J. B. Lippincott & Co., 1868.

_____. *The Principles and Objects of the Religious Reformation.* Bethany, W. Va.: Printed and published by A. Campbell, 1853.

Shackleford, John. *Life, Letters and Addresses of Dr. L. L. Pinkerton.* Cincinnati: Chase & Hall, 1876.

The Missouri Christian Lectureship. St. Louis: John Burns, Publisher, 1883.

Trible, J. M. *Trible's Sermons.* St. Louis: Christian Publishing Co., 1892, reprint.

Tucker, William E. *J. H. Garrison and Disciples of Christ.* St. Louis: The Bethany Press, 1964.

Willett, Herbert L. *Our Plea for Union and the Present Crises.* Chicago: The Christian Century Co., 1901.

PERIODICALS

American Christian Review (Indianapolis) 1858-1888.

The Christian Baptist, 1823-1830. Alexander Campbell, (ed.).

The Christian Messenger, 1826-1845. Barton Warren Stone and others, (eds.).

Christian Standard (Cincinnati: Standard Publishing) 1866. Founded by Isaac Errett.

The Disciple (St. Louis: Christian Board of Publication).

Gospel Advocate (Nashville) May 4, 1887.

Lard's Quarterly, Sept. 1863. "The Reformation for Which We Are Pleading."

Millennial Harbinger (Bethany, W. Va.) 1830-1870. Alexander Campbell, (ed.).

Mission Messenger (St. Louis) W. Carl Ketcherside, (ed.).

Restoration Herald (Cincinnati).

Restoration Review (Denton, Texas) n.d. Leroy Garrett, (ed.).

Scottish Journal of Theology, Sept. 1956.

PAMPHLETS AND ARTICLES

Creath, Elder Jacob. *A Tract on the Use and Abuse of Tobacco.* np: J. Sosey and Son, 1871.

Declaration and Address and The Last Will and Testament of the Springfield Presbytery. Indianapolis: International Convention of Disciples of Christ, 1949.

Errett, Isaac. *Our Position.* Louisville: William S. Broadhurst, n.d.

Fife, Robert O. "Christian Unity as Reception and Attainment." 1966 Reed Lectures. *Disciples and the Church Universal.* Nashville: Disciples of Christ Historical Society, 1967.

Harrell, David Edwin, Jr. "Peculiar People." 1966 Reed Lectures. *Disciples and the Church Universal.* Nashville: Disciples of Christ Historical Society, 1967.

Hayden, Edwin V. *50 Years of Digression and Disturbance.* Joplin, Mo.: Hunter Printing Co., n.d., ca. 1956.

Osborn, Ronald E. "Witness and Receptivity." 1966 Reed Lectures. *Disciples and The Church Universal.* Nashville: Disciples of Christ Historical Society, 1967.

Stone, Barton W. *History of the Christian Church in the West.* Lexington: The College of the Bible, 1956.

Stuckenbruck, Earl. *Sine Qua Non.* Private printing, n.d., ca. 1963.

Walker, Dean E. *The Tradition of Christ.* Milligan College Press, n.d., ca. 1963.

———. *Renewal Through Recovery.*

West. R. Frederick, and West, William Garrett. *Who Are The Christian Churches and What Do We Believe?* 1955.

Wilburn, Ralph G., "A Critique of the Restoration Principle," *The Restoration of Tradition.* St. Louis: The Bethany Press, 1963.

Wrather, Eva Jean. *Alexander Campbell and His Relevance For Today.* Nashville: The Disciples of Christ Historical Society, 1953.